NASTY WOMEN POETS

Nasty
WOMEN
POETS

An Unapologetic Anthology of Subversive Verse

Edited by Grace Bauer & Julie Kane

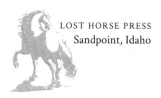

LOST HORSE PRESS
Sandpoint, Idaho

Grace Bauer's Author Photo: Mo Neal.
Julie Kane's Author Photo: Sean McGraw.
Book Design: Christine Holbert.

FIRST EDITION

This and other Lost Horse Press titles may be viewed online at www.losthorsepress.org.

LIBRARY OF CONGRESS CATALOGING-IN-PUBLICATION DATA

Names: Bauer, Grace, editor. | Kane, Julie, editor.
Title: Nasty women poets : an anthology of unapologetic verse / edited by Grace Bauer & Julie Kane.
Description: First edition. | Sandpoint, Idaho : Lost Horse Press, [2017]
Identifiers: LCCN 2017036576 | ISBN 9780998196336 (trade paper : alk. paper)
Subjects: LCSH: American poetry—Women authors. | Women—Poetry.
Classification: LCC PS589 .N26 2017 | DDC 811.008/09287—dc23
LC record available at https://lccn.loc.gov/2017036576

TABLE OF CONTENTS

SWEET INSPIRATION:
Nasty Women Poets on Foremothers & Role Models

MAMA SAID:
Nasty Women Poets on Mothers, Daughters & Growing Up Girl

PRETTY HURTS:
Nasty Women Poets on Beauty, The Body & Self-Image

WHAT'S LOVE GOT TO DO WITH IT:
Nasty Women Poets on Sex, Love & Lust

ROAR:
Nasty Women Poets on Bitches with Bad Attitudes

YOU DON'T OWN ME:
Nasty Women Poets on Talking Back to Men

HYMN TO HER:
Nasty Women Poets on Myths & Legends

SISTERS ARE DOIN' IT FOR THEMSELVES:
Nasty Women Poets on Sisterhood

SHE WORKS HARD FOR THE MONEY:
Nasty Women Poets on Work

PEOPLE HAVE THE POWER:
Nasty Women Poets on Social Justice & Political Protest

INTRODUCTION

If you have gone so far as to open this book after reading its title, we suspect you may, like us, have that moment from the final presidential debate still etched in your memory. Candidate Hillary Rodham Clinton was discussing Social Security when the opposing candidate (whose name we shall not utter here) interrupted her yet again, looking straight into the camera as he snarled, "Such a nasty woman!" While those old adages about people living in glass houses or pots calling kettles black may have entered your mind, you may also—like us, like many women and men—have felt an immediate sense of outrage, because you knew in your bones that in the candidate's mind, the epithet applied not just to his opponent on stage, but to any woman who had the audacity to stand up to him, contradict him, call him out in any way. Any woman who was not subservient, who refused to act like a pussy waiting to be grabbed, a model wife, or a Playboy bunny ready to serve. You may have taken it personally, or maybe you thought of your friends, mothers, daughters, wives, partners, sisters. Even if you were not a Hillary fan, you may have felt like a line had been crossed. So you were not surprised when the phrase quickly became a meme, a Twitter hashtag, a T-shirt women wore with defiant pride, commonly recognized shorthand for a critique of the sexism the insult embodied. The phrase stuck in our heads (as well as our craws).

As poets, we have always believed that writing well is the best revenge. We respond to language with language, our way of fighting fire with a brighter flame, so while we struggled to articulate our own responses, we had no doubt that other women poets were doing the same. What might happen if we asked to hear from them? And so the idea for this anthology was born. Our original call for poems read:

NOW IS THE TIME FOR ALL NASTY WOMEN POETS
TO COME TO THE AID OF THEIR COUNTRY

We are seeking poems from women who proudly celebrate their own nastiness and that of other women who have served as nasty role models. We want poems by and about women defying limitations and ladylike expectations; women refusing to be "nice girls;" women embracing their inner bitch when the situation demands it; women being formidable and funny; women speaking to power and singing for the good of their souls; women being strong, sexy, strident, super-smart and stupendous; women who want to encourage little girls to keep dreaming. If you are a woman who refuses to submit, we want to read your submission.

We planned from the start to post the call on Election Day—back when we still thought we might have reason to celebrate. When the unthinkable happened, we were almost too dismayed to proceed, but our feisty publisher, Christine Holbert, insisted the project was more important than ever—so the call went out a day after the election, with Inauguration Day as the deadline. With such a narrow window for submissions, we relied primarily on social media—posting and reposting on Facebook and Twitter and encouraging friends and followers to repost and share with their friends and followers, on their websites and in their blogs. While many of the nasty women poets we know are out there surely missed our call, by the deadline we'd received submissions from more than five hundred poets from across the U.S. and several foreign countries. Space limitations forced us to make some very tough decisions, but we are proud of the collection of voices we have compiled. They are part of a chorus that includes not just poets and writers, but artists in every genre (including the singers and songwriters who inspired our section titles), and women in various fields and factories, workplaces and walks of life who have, throughout history, stood their ground. Resistance takes many forms.

As with the historic Women's March on Washington (and other cities across the country and world), each contributor has her own reason for wanting to be part of this project. Some want to celebrate or pay homage, some want to rant and rage, some want to confront and some to confess, some want to kiss and some want to kick ass.

We editors came of age as young poets during the second wave of the Women's Movement, when the first women's poetry anthologies were appearing on the scene: *Rising Tides* (1973), *No More Masks* (1973), and *We Become New* (1973) among them. Those landmark anthologies inspired us, assured us that women's poetic voices mattered—even as the canonical anthologies used in our college classes said they did not. Later critical studies, such as Alicia Suskin Ostriker's *Stealing the Language: The Emergence of Women's Poetry in America* (1986) and others, began to put that work into its own canonical context.

Pages foxed with age, glued bindings cracking, those early feminist anthologies still occupy a space of honor on our bookshelves. But little did we suspect, more than four decades later, that the need for a women's poetry anthology would once again become compelling. We are especially moved by the fact that Marge Piercy (who contributed to all three of those 1973 anthologies) and Alicia Ostriker contributed to this one, as well—still fighting the good fight, as are the many other established, emerging, and unapologetically subversive women poets included here. While we might despair of the need for this collection, we choose instead to delight in its glorious nastiness and hope that its readers will, too.

Grace Bauer and Julie Kane
Editors

SWEET INSPIRATION:

Nasty Women Poets on Foremothers & Role Models

Patsy Asuncion

MATH FOR GIRLS COUNTS

Before they were great-great-grandmothers, they stood
in lines for singular equality, for one scale blind
to gender, creed or color. But, their right

to vote was delayed until 1920—144 years after
propertied White men, 51 years after Black men,
as if women were mere household amenities
used as conveniences.

The vote hoped to move the line closer
to a public voice in fiscal and sexual values,
but it took sixteen more years to change
birth control methods from *obscene*

to legal mail (hidden in plain brown envelopes)
to head-of-the-household husbands,
a married man the only
Good Housekeeping Seal of Approval.

Connecticut's 1965 defeat freed the pill
only for the sanctified wedded. I remember
unmarried, pregnant girls,
shamed and blamed for bad choices,
while boys were just being boys.

The 1982 ERA defeat subtracted sixty years
of female rights. One hundred years since suffrage,
fifteen states still have not ratified ERA,
now a dusty museum piece.

Defeat meant I had no credit, no bank account,
no property without my husband's name, addressed as
Mrs. John Doe, my first name unimportant,
a nondescript dustpan beneath spousal steps.

The recent Hobby Lobby Act fractionalized
1973's Roe vs. Wade by granting corporations
religious rights to reduce reproductive choice,
lost winnings to poker cheats.

Despite the centuries-old male monopoly,
women have done the math—
equal means equal, not less than.

GERALDINE FERRARO HAS BLOOD CANCER

While I blot my eyes, I tell her, "Geraldine Ferraro
Has blood cancer." She blinks twice, wets her lips,
And asks, "Who is Geraldine Ferraro? Oh, yeah."
For her, it's a lesson memorized for a final exam

That has blood cancer. She blinks twice, wets her lips.
I am odd, old, and now crying in front of her. Whatever.
For her, it's a lesson memorized for a final exam,
Not a rock star tragedy, not the last scene of the movie.

I am odd, old, and now crying in front of her. Whatever.
She has no inkling, none, what it was like—
Not a rock star tragedy, not the last scene of the movie—
When they wouldn't have made me boss, and she—

She has no inkling, none, what it was like
Before, when I waited tables in pinch-toe pumps, no degree,
When they wouldn't have made me boss, and she—
She would have been a waitress, too, or a stenographer.

Before, when I waited tables in pinch-toe pumps, no degree,
Maybe I would have wondered, "Who is Susan B. Anthony?"
She would have been a waitress, too, or a stenographer,
Another sitcom mom, pearl necklace and a chrome blender.

Maybe I would have wondered, "Who is Susan B. Anthony?"
But I switched on the televised convention and got switched on,
Another sitcom mom, pearl necklace and a chrome blender
In the commercial before the crowd went wild weeping.

I switched on the televised convention and got switched on,
Living my whole life packaged in a low-ceiling flat
In the commercial before the crowd went wild weeping,
And I wept, too, gasping the fresh air, but not even liking her,

Living my whole life packaged in a low-ceiling flat,
since she was New York, Mafia entourage, and some nerve,
And I wept, too, gasping the fresh air, but not even liking her,
Because the cage cupping my whole ambition swung open at last.

She was New York, Mafia entourage, and some nerve—
My mother had scolded, "Cross your legs. Sit like a lady,"
But the cage cupping my whole ambition swung open at last—
She had a narrow, nasal voice, said nothing I remembered.

My mother had scolded, "Cross your legs. Sit like a lady.
Don't let him know you are smarter than he is. Quiet."
She had a narrow, nasal voice, said nothing I remembered
Without wincing, but a black battalion of cameras shuttered,

"Don't let him know you are smarter than he is. Quiet,"
At the nominee, but she seemed as nonplussed as a future postage stamp,
Without wincing, but a black battalion of cameras shuttered,
And I was screaming, then howling into the sofa cushions in relief

At the nominee, but she seemed as nonplussed as a future postage stamp
By my reaction half the country away from her. I was ransomed,
And I was screaming, then howling into the sofa cushions in relief.
At least somebody showed them I could do it; a girl could do it.

My reaction half the country away from her: I was ransomed;
I went back to school, moved into the city, told nobody why.
At least somebody showed them I could do it. A girl could do it.
I got this job, got promoted. I became boss, and then the news.

". . . I went back to school, moved into the city, told nobody why,"
While I blot my eyes, I tell her. "Geraldine Ferraro . . .
I got this job, got promoted. I became boss, and then the news."
She asks, "Who is Geraldine Ferraro? Oh, yeah."

Stacey Balkun

LOOKING UP

How would orbit affect your ovaries,
your temper, they wondered. They doubted

a woman in space but you, Sally, your blue
NASA suit held your body renamed *courage.*

A crater bears your name on the moon.
How could they ask if you *wept*

when things go wrong on the job? I wish
I could have met you, begged

you to tell how it felt—floating
in zero gravity. We still gape, unable

to understand, our necks tilted back
as if we're still watching the shuttle burn.

Carol Barrett

MILK

For Alice Evans (1881-1975), who discovered
brucellosis, a disease carried by bacteria in fresh milk.
Her work was disparaged for years by Theobald Smith.
Like Marie Curie, she contracted the disease she studied.

It is in the milk, I tell them, the milk:
the goats on Malta, all the young
British recruits away from their own island
for the first time, buried on rocky cliffs
the goats hug in the fog.
It is in the milk, I tell them:
the swine losing their unborn
children in red clay. Afternoons
I bicycle up the hill along the fence
counting the dead with each press
of each pedal. It is in the milk
that goes into hard cheese, that feeds
our cousins in Wales, in Pennsylvania,
that makes them cough and sweat
and call us home. They won't
listen. I know the cause
of these ailments: a monster,
this small, can be dealt with.
All these lives, the most common
breakfast is danger, a runaway train
coming on fast; I alone know how
to work the brakes. Stop
the milk, I tell them, the milk.

Theo, you tiger, have a child
for God's sake, watch her choke

on your arrogance. Dairymen
you disown me, stranger in your field,
I who traipsed over long grasses,
watched the cattle fainting,
your wives with cold washrags
Sunday evening. I have drawn milk
from your cows' udders with my own
hands. I have tasted this infection.
Twenty-three years I have been telling you
how we become ill. You stand by,
animals nuzzling your waist,
dying of a disease I can name,
chide me as a witch.

Anne Champion

INDIRA GANDHI SPEAKS TO NIXON

It's unpleasant, talking to men about war—
like a visit to the gynecologist, when you want
to ask, *Is there a woman I may speak to about these matters?*
But I am stuck with him, quipping about
the gray streaks in my hair, joking
about Frankenstein's bride, and I say, yes,
Mr. President, I was not made by God:
a political woman is always made by man.
Don't think I don't know what a man like him
says about me behind closed doors.
He'll call me a witch, maybe worse,
but witch is my favorite. If only
I had such power—I'd curse them,
give them all vaginas and let them fumble
as they try to rule with such a handicap.
To see Nixon in a dress, his looks under careful
scrutiny, what a fantasy. I admit it,
this is what I think of every time
we meet. I stare at the wall and imagine
Nixon painstakingly applying lipstick
to meet with me and I think,
Not this old hag again, nagging about Russia.
It's a shame we have to run the world this way,
under the fists of men with egos so frail
they start a war. Nixon will call me
a cunning fox, he'll say I suckered him again,
but we're both cursed: he'll ruin himself,
I'll rely on men to protect me from ruin,
and we know how that ends for a woman.
And when the men who loved me grieve
my death, they'll shed blood and not tears.

I scribble in my notebook, never meeting his stare,
and his voice finally stops, waiting
for me to fawn at him, and I look up:
How much longer must we speak, sir?

Kelly Cherry

ORIENTAL NUDE

She lay in light, as if a light-
weight coverlet had billowed down
over her to keep off the chill,
since she would not fool with nightgown
or kimono, and yet she seemed
so inscrutable she might have been
the author of a book called *Zen and*
The Art of Being Comfortable in Your Own Skin.

Christine de Pizan
translated by *Maryann Corbett*

BALLADE LXXVIII, from *CENT BALLADES*

This jealous husband! What are we to do?
I wish to God we could just skin the man
who keeps his narrow eye fixed on us so
we can't get close. If only we could plan
to throttle the old villain with a mean
garrote! the filthy, gout-foot shrivel-brain
who brings us so much anger, so much pain.

I want him strangled. I want wolves to chew
his flesh, the worthless, skulking ball-and-chain.
What is he good for but to hack and spew,
screw up his face and whinge, and hack again?
Love him? Ha! The devil himself would strain.
I hate him, wrecked and broken thing, old man
who brings us so much anger, so much pain.

He doesn't do a thing but stalk and stew
—oh, but he needs a beating, that baboon—
in his own house. Rattle him through and through.
Drub him, so he takes to his bed, and soon!
Send him downstairs without his walking cane—
straight down, that spy who lurks behind the screen
and brings us so much anger, so much pain!

Heidi Czerwiec

SELF-PORTRAIT AS BETTIE PAGE:
AUTOBIOEROTIC

You started innocently: first, a pair
of words that rhyme, a sweet pentameter
that left you wanting more. And so you wrote,
for fun. And it was good. Someone took note
(young girl, new style) but thought you needed edge;
put you onto sonnets, with just a smidge
of sapphics—titillating, but still, quite tame.
You got a kick out of it. It was a game.

But then you got a penchant for harder stuff:
ballades, rondeaux—those French ticklers not enough
for you—you published hard-core villanelles
for magazines with certain clientele.
You're verse's vixen. Where do you go from here?
You keep composing; or, you disappear.

Anna Evans

DEAR SARAH RABBIT

Legend has it you were poaching, caught
your ankle in my great-grandfather's snare.
Then, when he knifed the rope, you spat and fought,
not like the local girls—black eyes, black hair.
Throwback, my mother always labeled me,
to your wild branch of my father's family tree.

So I invoke you like a ritual token
of my un-Anglo-Saxon-ness. In Spain,
I was addressed in Spanish. I've been spoken
to in Arabic and Hebrew. You explain
this, and those dreams, a weird prophetic lens
I can't speak of because it won't make sense.

Oh! I'm witchily glad you're my exotic
inside a vault of worthy Englishwomen.
It seems that I taste spicily erotic—
perhaps that's you too: coriander, cumin.
Whenever I bridle, question or rebel,
I hear you whisper your supportive spell.

What was it like for you, penned by four walls,
nursing my ancestor's ungrateful brats,
nights when the moon hung low and screech owl calls
stirred up your blood to hunt with the wild cats?
You knitted, or stitched in silence by the fire,
where flames died in the grate like mute desire.

Maria Mazziotti Gillan

MOLL FLANDERS, ZIA LOUISA, AND ME

Ah, Moll Flanders, of all the characters
in those novels I read when I was still young and in grad school,
it's you I remember,
flamboyant, sensual, in love with life.

You always looked for the "Main Chance"
and I, who can barely remember a name
five minutes after I hear it, remember yours.

I knew you were self-serving, but I loved
that you never lied about it,
that you never made excuses for your behavior,

and I imagine you trying to make your way
in 17th Century England, where a woman on her own
would have been vulnerable and afraid.

You remind me of my Zia Louisa,
        that woman who married four times,
        that woman who wore
                a tan-colored corset with lace stays
                that had to be pulled tight to hold in
                her large breasts and belly,
        that woman who loved to dance the Tarantella,
                her whole body exhilarating
                in moving and stomping.

And though I know Moll only through a male writer's portrayal,
I know Zia Louisa from my childhood,
knew her from watching her move
like an iron-sided battleship through life,

past three dead husbands and onto a fourth,
handsome, elegant Zio Guillermo.

They lived in the small apartment above us
on 17th Street in Paterson, NJ.
My mother told me that in the night she'd hear
Zia Louisa crying, but in the morning
she'd come down the back steps,
her cotton dress stiff with starch,
her lace handkerchief tucked in her sleeve,
and she'd be smiling and laughing.

She never told my mother
what sorrow she carried hidden in her sleeve.

The world does not need to know;
it only wants to pretend nothing is wrong,
nothing is wrong, and you are mistaken
if you think you heard wild sobbing
in the night.

Brittany Hailer

OPRAHFICATION

Originated by The Wall Street Journal in 1997
to describe public confession as a form of therapy

Another man left me the day after I turned 26
and Oprah turned 62.
After the balloons popped. After he and I took shot for shot.
After he produced a blue rubber dildo and slid.
After he smiled, held me down, took my ass and passed out.
After I cried sticky. After I threw up and threw
the lube across the wooden floor.
After the morning. After when he said he was done.
After he slammed the front door and I stumbled down the attic stairs.
After Stedman came in Oprah's bedroom with a breakfast tray.
After Gail called her to sing Happy Birthday.
After "You get a car! And you get a car! And you get a car!"
After Oprah licked the icing from her finger, sticky and sweet.

After Oprah was raped at age nine in rural Mississippi.
After I was raped at sixteen in a cement garage in Southern Maryland.
After *The National Enquirer* ran the story of her trauma
in 1990, the year I was born.
After the yellow-haired news anchors checked their lipstick.
After the lights came on and the cameras rolled.
After the blue TV shined on my mother's pregnant belly.
After she said it was time.
After the incision was made and I was pulled out of my mother.
After the doctor forgot the epidural.
After my mother screamed and shook.
After I was lifted, fondled,
touched for the first time
by the hands of a man.

After my mother saw her daughter
for the first time
in the arms of someone else.
After the first thing I knew
was to be taken by a stranger.
After I was handed back.

Kathleen Hellen

LOVE MISDEMEANORS

So you were Scarlett slapping Rhett.
Gilda in the role that ruined Hayworth.

No one was confused. No one was arrested.

"Let's all be manly," Hepburn said.
When Tracy shoved, she shoved back.

No one acted
to be correct.

The vixen Harlow even cracked:
"Do it . . .
again."

But somewhere in the recesses
of fear you know

you came that close.
It happens quickly.

He swagged a knife and said,
It would be easy.

This wasn't Baron slapping
Garbo for the first time.

Stanwyck said
she wanted him dead.

Elizabeth Lara

AIRPORT SECURITY

Ancient granny
drags her bag
gasping, wheezing
towards the gate
Security will let her wear
her shoes

She throttles and snorts
flings her purple
pocketbook onto the belt
slings her steel-plated
bangle beads
into the bin, from her

carry-on she pulls out
a can of Lysol spray,
her Chinese star and brass
knuckles, her newly
sharpened meat cleaver
She reaches into her

cleavage, gasps, extracts
an ice pick. The TSA officers
are trying to speak
She isn't finished yet
drops her winter coat
and furry ski vest into the

bin, unbuckles her color-
coordinated crocodile
leather belt
Behind her a crowd

is building up
The TSA is sending for

reinforcements
She pulls off her
turtleneck,
the sleeves
gesture skyward
She drops her purple

skirt to the floor,
pirouettes in her
purple Playtex Ultimate Lift
and Bali One Smooth U brief
Yee-hah
She flips the Chinese star

into the machinery
The crowd divides into
pros and cons
When she picks up
the meat cleaver
they scatter

She offers the agents
a swig from her
three-ounce bottle
of Smirnoff's
On the other side
of the metal detector

a TSA 20-something
is staring at her large
brass navel ring
The alarm bleats, she rasps
Pat me down, sonny
Pat me down

A MOMENT OF TRIBUTE

Hey, ever notice how
women used to fall
like small republics
on the movie screens
of America? We'd have
the sobbing heroine
fleeing through swamps
or jungles, a parking lot,
or the zoo at midnight.
with a spy, husband,
werewolf, man in black,
or free-lance nutcake
in competent pursuit;
and always, the poor dope
would take a tumble

over a box hedge,
or hit a gopher hole
and pull up lame
so those bad hombres
could snatch her up.
Even when the ground
was flatter than
Paul Newman's abdomen,
Miss Ineptitude would
still go sprawling
ass over acting lessons,
and even Snow White
in the big cartoon
had to meet with every
anthropomorphic root

in the enchanted forest.
For our relief we owe
the trimmest thanks to
actress Raquel Welch
(a.k.a. "Rocky) who
pioneered the art of
staying on one's feet.
I can assure you, after
hours of late night
research, that this
female piston galloped
through movie after
movie without tripping
once, and on occasion
she also turned round

and kicked her pursuer
in the stomach, or
whatever the censors
would permit; and now
we have women all over
dropping gangsters
and lighting zombies.
So pause, escapees,
briefly on your feet for
our forerunner Raquel,
who dodged the KGB,
bulls, dogs, pterodactyls,
and enormous corpuscles;
whose spirit, breasts,
and hemline never fell.

ROCK 'N' ROLL FEVER

for Joan Jett

As a child, she refused to play "On Top of Old Smokey,"
like all the girls. Instead she made us fall in love

with her androgynous cords, slim hips. She snorted coke
in airplane bathrooms, plopped

into a first-class seat, aviators shrouding her face.
She raised me, never wild as I thought,

but enough to brag even now that I ate mushrooms slathered
in peanut butter. Dosed on LSD from a dropper.

I used to drink pink tequila in my leopard cowboy hat. I wanted
anything the human spirit could throw my way,

so long as I could stand at its shining white center. Now,
I wear a ring on my left hand. Now I've buried

my first impulse in the desert of my parched frontal lobe.
I would've loved to keep crossing degrees

of risky latitude. Until, a few years ago, while driving drunk,
my girlfriends and I clipped

a parked car's side-view mirror and sent a smattering of glass
freckles into my face. I was leaving behind a trail

of shimmering wreckage. Even Joan had grown up: her blood
no longer sang with pills, her eyes

not lit up like twin bonfires. So, I said *stop the car.* Hailed
a taxi home. I sank into my claw-foot tub filled with ice.

When I woke, I thought I was no longer burning. Now, years later,
I listen to her, and wonder, what if all women

cool down with time? Or do we threaten to flap our rosy
flames through vents? I can only pretend this room

isn't smoking. I can only fan this fire away, as if to say,
goodbye for now.

WOMEN'S LIB

Women turned their loyalties from their father's clothes,
    huge discarded shirts.
They had been missing.

All night dreaming the map of the future their subject had been
    the artist at work
in a room under the stable.

It is vital to pull yourself up by your own roots.

We were making love in the weeds, slamming the dahlias flat.
Milkweed swollen then bursting. Outside birds.

Mostly the television is on, but we didn't notice.

We went to the movies.
Someone in the back row touched my arm
"Let them eat cake." And then I got angry.

Feathery trees embroidered on batiste:
old clothes in a poetic mode passed out of fashion.

Blessed be the womb put to use or not. Now dance.

Monica Rico

STOLEN AND UNNAMED

When my grandma died
her sister brought Mexico
in her pocket

a bag full of dirt
and sand that the chickens
hadn't run over
too much

small handfuls
of home
gunpowder residue
from the pistol she
slept with, beneath a pillow.

I was there to hear the voices
chanting as if on a train

towards Mexico, handkerchiefs
like doves resting and wrapped
in worn rosaries that remember
the last time they saw their sister
young. *¡Qué bonita San Louis Potosí!*

she said, no permission given
to her cousin
a thief and a husband.

Michoacán to Michigan where her
eyes became bullets or tulips
in the one photo I have

those same eyes I did not address
as *abuela,* too scared to lean in for one kiss,
a shiny blood line hidden in my throat

when she laughed
and said, I needed to be tamed, stolen,
and unnamed to taste this food.

HORSE FAIR

after "The Horse Fair," by Rosa Bonheur (1822–1899)

In men's clothes,
she makes herself
invisible to examine
anatomy at
the slaughterhouse.
She obtains
a police permit
to wear trousers
while she sketches.

At the horse fair,
she draws horses
pulling, snorting,
heads bumping,
thrashing, hooves
pounding, tails wringing,
charging forward,
rearing, bucking, wheeling,
disappearing into darkness.

Hooves hammer, whips
crack, horses writhe
between seer and seen,
the fairground a battleground.
Frenzied pitch, cymbals
clash, arms flail, whips
raised against the horses' arched
and shining necks.
Eyes bulge, terrified—
the dappled gray, the roan pull
away, toward thunder.

Lynne Thompson

SWING LOW, FREE

for Harriet

As scout and spy, nurse and train,
swing low, I went back south over
and over and brought them out.

Massa Brodess tried to sell me.
He failed. I turned runaway, after;
fled north and flaunted rules men

made to foil our liberty; led my kin—
ma and pa—from the land of black-
eyed Susans. I could not save all

who bled my blood but I led multitudes
from Bucktown to Cambridge, Camden
to Blackbird, trusted in Bakongo mojo

(*nkisi makolo*), relied on Xhosa charms
and the Igbos' blue and white codes hung
from oaks, on doors, on countless quilts

along the way; their patterns steering us
north by stitch; Shoofly, Log Cabin, Bear's
Paw, Wagon Wheel, sweet-swinging from

porticoes in Dover, in Smyrna and Odessa,
our field guides to the Choptank River,
a cipher of bedclothes draped for an uppity

Moses, *o sweet chariot.* I would live free
or die. When I took the freedom and
looked at my hands, I knew I had to be

the same breaker of laws in Newcastle and
Wilmington, Chester County and beyond,
where I brought them up, brought them out

to the Eastern shore where a mighty Jehovah
was troublin' the waters of slaveholders who
named me Araminta; slave-drivers who put

a bounty on my head. Descended from
Ashanti, I remembered Anansi, West
Africa's trickster, followed the Drinking

Gourd and stole away to Jesus on Whirlpool
Bridge, Canada, where I looked over Jordan.
I had help. Fred Douglas and William Still

and many Quakers, who were almost as good
as coloured, and could be trusted every time
to burn bright the candlelight in their garrets.

Always, I went back. Died, March 10th.
Crossed over, free. Today I'm lauded and
immortalized, roots of struggle stitched

on my bustle, faces of unnamed risk-takers
tatted on the skirt of a scout, spy, nurse,
train, a woman singing *we mean to live free.*

Kathrine Varnes

THE BRA BURNERS

You know those little blowtorches chefs use to caramelize the sugar
on your crème brûlée? That's how you know a professional,

one who loves the stench of smoldering Lycra, knows just when
   to give it another blast.
It takes a steady hand to singe the little bow first, experience

to understand to start the straps early and back off any foam padding,
patience to get the underwires charred to just the right smoky black

that even Georgia O'Keeffe wouldn't mind painting.
It's expensive as a habit. I suggest for your first time to offer a bra
   with bulky seams,

bad lace, elastic starting to pucker. That way, the snap of release
from the hooks will feel right; no regrets as you pull your elbow
   through one loop,

then the whole contraption out through your other sleeve.
   Look at it—dangling
between your pinched thumb and finger. How truly awkward

it is without you. How gangly and wrong.
The performance burners are another thing, not just about
   providing a service.

I've seen them use hibachis, fondue pots, gas ranges, a pack
   of cigarettes,
fry daddies, hot-wired electrolysis machines, crossed jumper cables,
   curling irons,

kilns, vanilla scented candles, university-owned Bunsen burners,
  a shot of brandy
flambé, magnifying glasses on a sunny day, even easy-bake ovens.

You might mistake a few as amateurs at first, pulling out
  a big red box
of kitchen matches like cub scouts building their first fire.

But when Janice leaves the bra on and presses the pink hot
  match tip to the satiny cup,
you settle into your metal folding chair, the sweat on the back
  of your thighs,

and watch the transformation, the delicate pointillism revealing
  a flower, the figure
of a real woman, your mesmerized face.

Natasha T. Wall

YOUNG BLACK HISTORIAN (GRANDFATHER'S GARAGE)

I read it in an old book
when I was very young.
Somethin' 'bout the *pateroller*
and how "they" was on the run.
The lines? They read like scripture
and the rhythm fried like sun.
Teachin' history things to girl
when I was very young.

Pick up the chant and hear the roar
of each embracing line.
Feel music in your bone and grit
and stamp your foot in time.
Don't ever catch the colored man,
you *pateroller* pig!
But always keep him on the run
or else the leaves were rigged.
'Cuz it's not the catch, just the chase
that makes my Africa strong.

Still hearing murmurs from the whelps
when I was very young.

Janet Lee Warman

PANTHER AND JAGUAR

The Panther and the Jaguar are beasts of two different species
and the Jaguar's natural habitat is up cheerful trees.

—*Letter from H.G. Wells to Rebecca West*

Cheerful trees are extinct in this wood
where every panther's cry
is met with jaguar moan.
A forest of derision is no home for me.

When I sent baby Anthony to London
to be out of the way of bombs
and fretted when they fell on Harley Street,
you called me hysteric.

When I fell into a polluted well,
my septic hand turning blacker by the day,
you prepared for a Czechoslovakian lecture
and called me hypochondriac.

When your friend Hedwid
slit her wrists in your dining room,
I hushed the press, then found she was far more than friend.
You called me paranoid.

Call me panther when you wish to woo me.
Send me drawings of your paw entwined with mine.
But do not call me panther when you shun me.
I long to sharpen claws on tender bark.

PENNYROYAL

Pennyroyal doesn't last in public parks.
Plucked in the dark, its roots infused in tea,
it does the moon's work pulling the dark tides
within the body. Women know it well.

Men hadn't been distinguished from the apes
a full two weeks before they had invented
intoxicating drinks. Murder and rape
followed, as well as fire and the wheel.

The women countered strength with wiliness.
Power was in the roots and leaves they stewed
and simmered, knowledge gathered seed by seed
while men ignored the damp world underground.

What men brew make them heroes, and what women
brew makes them witches, quick to burn. We do
our work in darkness, in the kingdom of
the healing roots, the diamond mines, the dead.

Jin-Jin Xu

THE TRACTOR

In a tractor he came for her. She waited, the lone passenger; the engine broke through the air—from behind the horizon, its steady breath closed in, plowed the earth to her ear.

In an oversized blue suit he came for her: cotton dress, purse clutched to chest, hair swept up by an ox-bone clip.

Her wedding—an imagined spectacle. Slurred vows; foreheads banging against ground to fathers & uncles & grandfathers & the dead; a drunken game to steal the bride.

Here, she stole onto a train. No goodbyes, she stepped on & stepped off onto the platform of dirt and dust.

The engine, the engine—she listened, waiting for a life outside the choke of mosquito netting, the blank walls of her room. One by one, her sisters had left, where was there to hide, last daughter of the house?

With a dead mother, a daughter is a body with a price.

In a tractor he came for her. She listened, a seashell to her ear.

MAMA SAID:

Nasty Women Poets on Mothers, Daughters & Growing Up Girl

Janet E. Aalfs

QUEER

When my mother at the table noted
the roast tasted queer,
I watched my father stare
as if to freeze the air
that sizzled like spit
on an iron skillet
    and disappeared.
No one saw me
    gone.
Every nerve and current spoke
    invisibly true.
Like the slap he had meant
to stop a boy
from kissing me, or worse,
the girl he did not see, silent
lips to mine.
I trusted every feeling.
    My ground.
    My spine.
And learned the meaning
of mercy then—love
blessed that word my choking
parents swallowed to live.
    And pierced my heart.
    And pushed me out.

Devon Balwit

I WANT TO MANTLE MY DAUGHTERS' BODIES

I want to mantle my daughters' bodies
stand pugnacious at the doorways of their ears, their sexes
snatch arrows of derision mid-arc, no wounds shall come of them

I want to slide between my daughters and their lovers
wrap arms around those enfolding them, whisper *careful, do no harm,*
give her pleasure, my hands ready threats by testicle and jugular

I want to form testudo around all daughters on all streets
clack shield and spearpoint, lay ambush, leave the bodies of rapists
    and molesters
for dark birds to consume

I want to enter their blood, coursing and flowing,
give them pride in its nature—this red thread stitching generations,
this ancient libation, enfleshed, elemental

I want to prove to my daughters that, though they bleed,
they are world makers, atom smashers, pleasure seekers,
    pleasure takers,
claimants of every right due thinking-kind

"ELEGANT," SHE SAID

My new friend was chuckling, saying she cracked up when I let fly
with the "f" word while speaking to an audience
    of five hundred because, she said, I look so "elegant, a class act,
a knockout." I changed the subject. She doesn't
    get it. In the Bean family, I was the clumsy one, by sixth grade
inhabiting a close-to-six-foot, rib-protruding,
    hunched-over frame, buck teeth in braces, wispy blonde hair, pale
bluish eyes. Called "Scarecrow" and "String Bean" by
    other kids. "Boobless Bean," my nickname in high school. And
with a regal-shouldered, chocolate-eyed, russet-haired
    mother who modeled for the fashion pages of *The Tucson Daily
Citizen.* My brunette little sister: "the pretty one":
    began Flair Modeling School at fourteen. Those 1950s
Clairol ads: "Do blondes have more fun?" Not me—
    I didn't measure up. The time I brought my drawing of a girl
to show Daddy and his only comment was a clipped,
    "She's not very pretty." Over my parents' Old Fashioneds,
banter about women: "pert little nose, a shame
    about her piano legs;" "good-hearted, but that horrendous
pitted skin." Now the flesh of my arms droops
    like crumpled silk. Yet my husband swears he loves
my bones. Once, when Mom was around my age,
    she spoke of her granny Lilian Walker Graves, who sparkled
on the vaudeville stage. "I've told you she was
    a beauty, simply stunning," Mom said, adding that men tripped
on their shoe strings at the sight of her. "And my
    own mother," she went on, "had that same quality, just as I did,
and—as your little sister does," she added,
    looking at the ceiling. But then, the year before Mom died
in the retirement home, as I walked beside
    her electric cart while she steered past wheelchairs and

walkers, a resident stopped us: "Why Pam,"
she gushed, "This daughter of yours—no one would question
you're her mother! She looks just like you,
moves with your elegance, your grace." Mom jerked upright
and sputtered, "She *does*?" and pressed her foot
on the accelerator, whizzing off. I had to run to keep up with her.

SCAR SEASON

As a girl I wanted one, simple,
uninterrupted, those zags
of tell and hide: injury, surgery,
the open and closed mouth
of them all at once.

After my friend fell from her bike,
she had lines tied into her chin,
little shocks of thread that poked
their spikes when I touched them.

I did not think about the blood,
the needles, how she wailed
at the split, how my hands covered
the gap as I stumbled her home.

All I saw was the glare of accident
on her skin, the remarkable way
they fixed her, how her face stayed
together when she smiled, screamed.

I told no one why I raced my Schwinn
down Dead Man's Hill, why I jumped
from the dare tree, roller-skated into the ravine.

I grew lonely over the bruises and scrapes,
the adornments that healed and disappeared,
the betrayal of Band-Aids.

Then: chicken pox. The threat of my body
tied to itch, my mother photographing

my marked back, stunned
at the terrific colonies of red.

Don't, everyone said, when I touched
them. *You will scar.* And I thought
of the bike, the falls, the skates sitting
barren. And all I had to do was release,

lift the scab each time it formed until finally,
on my ankle, a round crater,
a universe to claim: the scar without

the accident, the mark without the wound,
how I was simply given
what I tried so hard to create.

Cathleen Calbert

BAD GIRL ATTITUDE

The ... book ... everywhere proclaims its bad girl attitude ..."

—*Kirkus Reviews*

You mean *those* girls, don't you?
   The ones with broken-heart tattoos
      on their biceps, *fuck the world*
         on their fingers, snapping BlackJack,
            snapping the straps of black bras,
               heat-packing, cigarette-smoking,
                  drive-by-shooting homegirls,
               biker chicks, groupies, junkies,
           Nancy Spungen, *Poison Ivy,*
         thongs rising above low-cut jeans,
      navels pierced with gold rings,
   dresses more than three inches
above Catholic knees, girls who get
   blue highlights, girls who are blue
      light specials, Saturday night specials,
         K-mart queens, trailer trash, *Badlands'*
           Caril Fugate, Aileen Wuornos riding
              her bicycle toward a Florida highway,
            chicas, banditas, vandalistas,
         with razor blades in their teeth,
           giving head in Chevys, giving guys shit,
         skanks, sluts, hos, tramps who leave home,
   runaways on the Boulevard,
vampire princesses and little witches
   with their pentangles and love-me spells,
   girls who walk the tracks,
      who get into the back seat,

(*A hundred for five minutes*
the guy in a Caddy yelled at me),
Lolitas, prick teasers, Amy Fisher
at the door, girls in juvee, in jail,
on death row (in Texas, a future president
mocked Karla Faye: *Please don't kill me),*
girls sleeping in homeroom,
slamming boys into lockers,
hanging out in the park after dark,
on the upper level of the mall, at the end
of the alley, girls who have sex,
who write about having had sex, old girls
at the podium, at the mic, at the chalkboard,
holding onto youth and abuse (*Why not me?*
he asked when I was on acid in Palm Springs—
I'd known him since I was three),
girls who've done everyone but won't
do you. Is that what you mean? Listen,
I've got a tire iron, a pearl-handled pistol,
and a fast-tracking Macintosh. I'm not
a bad girl at all. I'm a bad woman,
and I am here to kick your ass.

Lauren Carpenter

REFUSING PARENTHOOD

Children press against the glass and watch two rat snakes
cruise through the peat and wood chips like model trains,
zigzagging towards a fake-rock tunnel
where in the dark people crowd the tracks and shout

Make your own babies, you can teach them anything,
they're like apple trees
        As if anyone can be a botanist, as if it's simple
        to graft branch to body, to strip away
        what makes bitter apples, spitters, pitted skins.
        As if it's easy to train a tree to grow along a wall.

Try it, you'd be great
        they say, as if it were a switch we could click
        to change tracks, to let our line jump forward.
        We could engineer ourselves, wear uniforms,
        learn to offer methodical schedules, accommodations,
        warm embraces at the station. They claim

this is what we were made for, and it'll happen anyway.
Happiness is a baby waving at a steam engine.
Stability is a wakeful night with its crown of dawn.
But a snake is not a train.

We emerge from the clacking tunnel, see the soft-edged children
behind the glass, and bob our heads at them. We turn away:
that is our memorial to the first fruit
and its twin, the empty hand. To choosing that.

SELF-PORTRAIT ON POP ROCKS

When I was born I was freaking awesome. My dad tells me I was all head and could cough for an entire night without stopping. By third grade I knew at least ten nursery rhymes. I could write my name in cursive. I learned my times tables in under three months. I understood what a hypothesis was within minutes of my teacher telling me. By junior high I was fluent in English, backtalk, and Midwest Caucasian. At fourteen I could rollerblade both backwards and forwards. At fifteen I could clear a sewer grate. Between 18 and 20, I learned to identify at least four reservoirs beneath the hood of a car, survived two weeks in a tent with nothing but a cooler full of food and a debit card, moved my T-shirt and CD collections into a dorm room, convinced a chemistry teacher to pass me, financed a mid-size car. After that I was unstoppable. I ate dinner in restaurants, shopped in produce departments, held short conversations at parties with average looking men, mini-golfed on weekends, slept in late on Sundays, repainted wicker furniture, nursed a cold sore, scrambled eggs with ease.

Patricia Clark

TOMBOYS

A word for girls who climbed trees,
          who shinnied up
     the rough bark not caring
               about skinned elbows and knees,
     who rode—too fast—on bicycles
down alleys rutted with gravel.

They refused to come in from the dark
          to their names
     called in a litany of names
               by mothers standing, almost
     forlorn, in lighted doorways.
I overheard Grandmother use the word

for me. Was it that year, or earlier,
          when I'd stood,
     summer tanned and ragged,
               slicking back my hair in the bathroom,
     imagining my face as a boy's?
Steve Kirby, Jimmy Georgia, Gregory Federighi.

In 1961, in Tacoma, what did I know
          of sexual politics?
     Grandmother was telling Mother
          I was disgraceful, a renegade.
     She recommended dresses, knitting,
less time with Father, less time outdoors.

And then, at school, Sister Gabrielle's words
          scalded my face.
     "Sit like a lady," she hissed,

and I tried to, knees together,
not knowing what I'd done wrong.
Why were the women so angry?

I've gone back, more than once, to the school
and the playground,
now predictably cramped and small.
Like a refugee in a war-torn country,
I escaped without a glance back, taking
only what I could grip in my hands, or remember.

Cathryn Cofell

WHAT HAPPENS WHEN DAD TELLS MOM TO SELL HER CAR

She changes her name to Josie,
lights a Slim 100, lets the top down,
pitches the For Sale sign
he stuck in the window after he proposed,
pitches her pantyhose like a bridal bouquet
on the way out of town.
She drives—
this creamy, leggy, black-haired Italian beauty—
in her lemon yellow convertible
and red polish. She keeps driving,
past the Ben Franklin, the post office,
St. Anne's Catholic Church.
She doesn't stop, doesn't even cool
the engine when she pauses for gas,
Paydays, more cigarettes,
a pair of rhinestone-studded cat eyes
and a leopard print scarf.
She doesn't stop until she hits ocean,
the Statue of Liberty.

She finds a studio in the Village
with an ex-stripper-turned-lounge-singer
named Shirlee, who needs an angle
and Mom is it—
the vixen and the virgin,
the sinner and saint—so Mom sells
the car to buy a warped upright
(she knows all those show tunes by heart),
and they make wispy music together,

two dames knocking out
"Someone To Watch Over Me" and
"What Kind of Fool Am I."
Shirlee and Josie pack the house,
they make men growl, they make men shift
in their tight polyester leisure suits.
These men,
they want to take Mom home,
smooth out her hair, buy her nice things,
give her the life she deserves.
Give her the life only a fool
would refuse.

Carla Drysdale

LIFTED, CARRIED

At nine, your son will find
the dildo nestled
in its shiny oblong box

underneath the folded winter
pullovers, he will lift it
from its molded plastic bed

peer through its rose silicon
skin to the two rings
of marble-sized metal balls

which rotate at a button's press,
he'll touch the tiny rabbit ears
at the base.

At 13, red-faced, brazen,
knowing its purpose now
he'll confront you,

you'll tell him there is no shame.
The body's hungers for pleasure
demand feeding

one way or another.
Still, he will sing out *dildo*
whenever he thinks of it

owning your secrets, just as you,
at nine, discovered her love
letters in her lingerie drawer.

Her shame ran wider
than the dirty waves
of Lake Erie licking the shore

in those blue and yellow summers
the waves lifted
and carried you swimming.

In winter, you climbed up
and over their cold
jagged shapes.

I DRINK AFTER MY KIDS ARE ASLEEP

Not too much, but just enough that the bright red
don't mess with mama curtain narrowly opens
like the bottom of a sloppy kid's shirt.

My husband and I do bad things on purpose.
We put our bare black feet on the table,
blast videos with comedians cursing,
throw booger snot tissues across the room,
miss the unclean garbage can and leave it
there until morning when my toddler wakes again
before dawn yelling, *Caci!* And I carry him

to the kitchen cloudy sky-eyed and see
the half empty baby blue bottle of tequila
sitting on the table from the night before

and I am reminded that beneath my bitch
tired bones is a woman who wears lipstick
and who, when her husband tosses her mustard
stained clothes to the floor, curses and fucks
and makes the baby monitor squeal
with her primordial life-making yell.

Sara Henning

OTHER PLANETS, OTHER STARS

At the shooting range, my mother and aunt
single out pistols, set aside an hour to palm
the grip of unversed steel, trigger guard,

every barrel's delicately latticed gorge.
And after, they inundate targets at their chakra points,
first head, then heart. Flare after flare

penetrating paper. Astronomers say that only one in five
stars like the sun hosts an earth-sized world,
but I can't stop thinking of the smaller planets,

gaunt and mysterious, little martyrs of rock
accelerating in circuit, wondering what's to come.
I'm quarantined in the lobby, a pair of muffs

sheathing my ears. I'm not old enough to fear
men who swagger through unlocked doors, to slip
a hand under the bed skirt night after night

like my mother every time our house moans
under a broken stud, discerning metal from ruche.
Not every world has the girth to sashay

against gravity, so it hoards what it can. Planets
pulverized to radiant dust become girls of panic
and stone. I watch through bulletproof glass

how my mother now mimes the length
of the pull, metal jacketing the bullet's scorching interior.
I want to be a planet far from this

sisterhood of Kepler data, where silhouettes
of men exert strong centrifugal force. I want
to be a soft glint of rock heralding her own

inertia, body without magnetic field
distorted by another celestial urging—aim the muzzle
like a solar tsunami. Detonate or run.

Andrea Holland

WEIRDO

She'd lined up a date with her mascara again
and it was only Tuesday. The way she looked

at herself in the mirror didn't stand up, but hey
no hickeys on her neck. At school they called her

freak. Her steel-toed boots left marks like skulls
on the walls as she passed the swim team

in the hall. The lockers shook and the Quarterback
rose up and passed a look along the line, the pack

itching to break her funny accent in, mess with that
weird hair, and a nose ring like a dolled-up bull.

She stared right back. By Friday, their red capes
of anger snapped.

Trish Hopkinson & Tyler Mills

WAITING AROUND

after "Walking Around" by Pablo Neruda

It so happens, I am tired of being a woman.
And it happens while I wait for my children to grow
into the burning licks of adulthood. The streaks
of summer sun have gone,

drained between gaps into gutters,
and the ink-smell of report cards and recipe boxes
cringes me into corners. Still I would be satisfied
if I could draw from language
the banquet of poets.

If I could salvage the space in time
for thought and collect it
like a souvenir. I can no longer
be timid and quiet, breathless

and withdrawn.
I can't salve the silence.
I can't be this vineyard
to be bottled, corked,
cellared, and shelved.

That's why the year-end gapes with pointed teeth,
growls at my crow's feet, and gravels into my throat.
It claws its way through the edges of an age
I never planned to reach

and diffuses my life into dullness—
workout rooms and nail salons,

61

bleach-white sheets on clotheslines,
and treacherous photographs of younger me
at barbecues and birthday parties.

I wait. I hold still in my form-fitting camouflage.
I put on my strong suit and war paint lipstick
and I gamble on what's expected.
And what to become. And how
to behave: mother, wife, brave.

Diane Kendig

BICYCLES PROPPED IN THE GARAGES OF MY LIFE

I would not waste my life in friction when it could be turned into momentum.

—*Frances Willard*

The garage door inches open on me, painting the frame
of the old bike I begged from my cousin, navy blue to match
the fenders I purchased from Sears Roebuck
and the pneumatic tires—I who never bought anything
and didn't really want a bicycle to ride.
What *did* I want it for at age 10?

Our road, as my mother pointed out, was too dangerous,
and the roads behind went nowhere. But her father
wouldn't allow her one, so she wouldn't deny me
like that, especially when the cousin was
her sister's daughter. That cousin was pregnant
by age 17 and never went anywhere.

The bike went on all my moves, as I got out of Canton,
Columbus, Vermillion, Oberlin, Cleveland, Findlay
then on to Rochester and ten years near Boston,
and back to Ohio where my city planner friend is back
decades later, with a job promoting our path for bikes,
and mine sits in storage, as it always has.

Committed to green, my friend, as I am,
still forty years of my life with a bike I never rode,
and wondered about till now, reading Susan B. Anthony,
who said the bike "has done more to emancipate women
than anything else in the world . . . ,
gives women a feeling of freedom and self-reliance."

I never needed a mountain, racing, or touring bike,
or cruiser, though I dreamed of a tandem
so I could ride and sing, "give me your answer, do,"
but loyally stuck with what I had, though I never named it,
like Willard, who named her bike "Gladys"
because it gladdened her,

the way the bikes of my life have gladdened me,
propped in my garages, ready if I ever needed them,
come gas shortage or no, and I could see myself,
as Anthony saw such girls as me,
"the picture of free, untrammeled womanhood."

Lucinda Lawson

ANOTHER BARBIE'S LOST HER HEAD

Ken, in obvious denial, parks himself straight-legged,
staring with a Dick Clark grin. His elbows
locked, his arms outstretched as if to stay
the trauma, he can't seem to take it in, but we knew

something had to give: her noodle's coy twist
and tilt, its folly more than such a slender
stem of neck could bear. No wonder
she snapped. My daughter drops her noggin

in my palm, and we inspect the corpse. She's
stripped, a stiffened rubber chicken; her white meat
could feed a dollhouse crew. We jam her pretty head
on tight. We twist and tamp it firm, and here

we have her new. She can look us
in the eye; she's bolder. So what if scarves
and turtlenecks obstruct her view?
She's got a good head on her shoulders.

ON THE LESSER-KNOWN USES OF
MEAT TENDERIZER

Once I began to menstruate at 13,
I rapidly became an expert at
expunging bloodstains from pajamas, jeans,
dresses, bedsheets, upholstery, even mats
and rugs. I'm ready for a life of crime
now, armed with skills ideally suited for
a career of carving finger-deep red lines
in victims' throats, disposing of their cars
in forested ravines. You need to learn
the art of covering your tracks before
making tracks, you must master how to burn
love letters prior to allowing your
mind to love, and you must know how to strike
the backspace key before you learn to write.

Kim Lozano

TAMPON DISPENSER

In the girls' bathroom of our school
the silver box hung there like it owned the place.
As invincible as an iron sink in a prison cell,
its fascist presence demanded we be women now,
its pink and aqua pictures insisted
we were supposed to like it.

When the door opened you could see it
from the hallway, and at the drinking fountain
the boys snuck peeks at that chamber
full of the strange little plungers
they'd examined in their mom's vanities.
They wanted to know what went on beyond that door
but were scared of getting too close
to that room, and that box,
stainless steel, impregnable—forever an alien ship.

PLAYING FOR KEEPS

I wanted the aggie. Delighted in the deep green
and red flow of it, how colors twisted
around its surface and gold shone,
like a princess's crown caught in moonlight,
when Ronny held it toward the sun.
I wanted it for keeps, but only peewees and
a blue boulder made it into my pouch.
"Not fair," I whined. And, then, "Okay.
If I have to." Sticking my thumbs
into the elastic waistband I wriggled
off my shorts and slipped
my yellow cotton underpants—
blue *Saturday* stamped near the hip—down
my skinny thighs. He had one minute
to stare at the smooth bare mound
split by a thin cleft before
handing over payment.

Jennifer Perrine

LETTER TO HALF A LIFETIME AGO

Dear girl waiting outside, alone,
　　just tossed out of your parents' house:
　　　　I offer this age's adage—
　　　　　　it gets better. Sometimes it does.
　　　　Other people's mothers will take
　　you in, admit the sin's to leave
a kid on the streets, but they'll turn,

too, when they find your fingers twined
　　in their daughters' hair. You'll seek bars
　　　　where you don't get carded, linger
　　　　　　under the beneficent reign
　　　　of queens who bring you to diners
　　in the wee hours, make sure you eat.
You'll play pool with butches who teach

you to flick your lighter open,
　　chivalrous, although you don't smoke,
　　　　how to shave your head when barbers
　　　　　　won't, what to do when men eye you
　　　　in a parking lot, hurl insults,
　　then rocks. You'll learn the exact size
of bruise left by a fist, the shape

of the girl who lifts you, carries
　　you to her car, her home, lets you
　　　　sleep while she cooks you eggs and toast.
　　　　　　She'll lend you book after book, whole
　　　　pages underlined, where you glimpse
　　worlds of two women together,
fictions where they do what they please

with their lives, and still they survive.
　　When she declares you *just a friend*,
　　　　you'll write your gloom and grief, won't cry.
　　　　　　You'll drink until your mind's scrubbed clean,
　　　　then test sobriety at clubs
　　where you press sweat to sweat to bass
and drums. You'll wear studded leather,

white tanks, black boots: signals that say
　　both *fuck off* and *come here*. You'll fall,
　　　　gob smacked, and they'll fall, too: broken
　　　　　　beauties, motorcycle chicks, punk
　　　　princesses, gynoanarchists.
　　Each time, you'll buzz with kisses
you wish wouldn't stop, embraces

in the midst of busy sidewalks,
　　bustle around you forgotten.
　　　　Each will leave you waiting, cast off,
　　　　　　alone again, but now knowing
　　　　this isn't the end, that you'll see
　　your way through with one long, steady
stride, and the next one, and the next.

Anne Delana Reeves

KAYLA'S COOL WORLD

Bored with cruising past the Skyline Drive-In,
past Tastee Freeze and Walmart's parking lot
where car radios scan stations of sugary pop
or Zeppelin's first chords to *Stairway to Heaven*,
she climbs the town's water tower,
a can of black spray to make her mark
above the glut of lights, matchbox cars,
and static hum of a junked-up world.
But what to write? Who does she love anyway?
Somewhere a supernova is dying,
too great to sustain its appetite for light.
She imagines that chaotic burst of flames.
The paint can hisses words that shine, like jewels,
fixed and whole. All her own. How cool.

Judith Sornberger

AT MIDLIFE, DOROTHY TALKS SENSE
TO HER DAUGHTER

In a weak moment I wished for the wrong thing.
Stunned by the slippers' ruby-tinted promise,
I forgot that home is prone to cyclones,
that I'd be buried like my mother
under the dustwhirl of seasons. Look at me:
a filthy apron over my faded pinafore,
my auburn braids twisted with iron.

I had my pick of straw men, tin men, munchkins.
I went for the tin, figured I had heart enough
for two, that I could give him what he needed.
That's how it begins, my pretty.
You love his hard chest, his tin soldier stiffness.
Next thing you know, you're thanking heaven
for the nights he's getting lubed down at the tavern.
Except when he bangs the empty drum of himself
all the way home and you know to duck and cover.

Trust me, you'll get no place mooning over rainbows,
for all their promises, but plunked back down
on the same depleted acre. Watch for thunderheads,
my girl, a witchy silhouette riding a broom.
Don't be a goody-two-shoes like your mother.
Hitch a ride into the wind.
Shriek and howl and never land.

A. E. Stallings

FOR ATALANTA

Your name is long and difficult, I know.
So many people whom we didn't ask
Have told us so
And taken us to task.
You too perhaps will wonder as you grow

And blame us with the venom of thirteen
For ruining your life,
Using our own love against us, keen
As a double-bladed knife.
Already I can picture the whole scene.

How will we answer you?
Yes, you were in a hurry to arrive
As if it were a race to be alive.
We weighed the syllables, and they rang true,
And we were hoping too

You'd come to like the stories
Of princesses who weren't set on shelves
Like china figurines. Not allegories,
But girls whose glories
Included rescuing themselves,

Slaying their own monsters, running free
But not running away. It might be rough
Singled out for singularity.
Tough.
Beauty will be of some help. You'll see.

But it is not enough
To be nimble, brave or fleet.
O apple of my eye, the world will drop
Many gilded baubles at your feet
To break your stride: don't look down, don't stoop

To scoop them up, don't stop.

Lisa Gluskin Stonestreet

GOOD

girl, and what of it? Pinned, filed, known,
noticing, noticing: she

some form of I, not-I. Disclaimer.
Entirely ordinary, talked out and down

to worn familiar, wrapped doll
lashed to a board. Seed-pearl stitches,

subtle sheen. How to seem,
to be, nothing again.

Remember the red leatherette,
the silver buckle? O Maryjane, your strap

across my instep. I just wanted
to hold you up to the light.

I not-I. Having it both ways. The woman
in the next cubicle, scuffed heel of her shoe.

And at what point, please god
might I come to love the falling, long roll

down the hill? Twigs in my hair.
Good enough. Good. Enough.

Marilyn L. Taylor

HOW AUNT EUDORA BECAME
A POSTMODERN POET

A girl is not supposed to write that way
(the teachers told her in the seventh grade)—
you ought to find more proper things to say.

For instance, there's no reason to portray
your daddy sucking gin like lemonade—
young girls are not supposed to write that way.

And we don't care to read an exposé
on how your mama gets the grocer paid;
there ought to be more proper things to say.

Why not write about a nice bouquet
of flowers, or a waterfall, instead?
You cannot be allowed to write the way

you did, for instance, when your Uncle Ray
was entertaining strangers in his bed,
and what the county sheriff had to say.

Why put such vulgar passions on display?
You're going to regret it, I'm afraid—
remember, you're a girl. So *write* that way.
Go find yourself some proper things to say.

Kim Tedrow

TORNADO DREAMS

Now I learn it was a thirty-five-foot muslin sock that tore
on the first take, was mended with music wire and suspended
from a gantry as it stalked the poor girl on the Kansas prairie.
Caught in the cool calm center of the storm, the girl watches
ousted bits of the world ride the wind: a chicken coop, two guys
in a rowboat, livestock, and an old woman on a bicycle,
    all accompanied
by light orchestral music. I was three when I saw the movie,
took the storm to bed, slept and howled next to the fan
that ran in reverse to pull the heat from the second story bedrooms.
Over decades the dreams have changed but the storm is the same:
the world is loud and out of order, sirens wail from the outside in.
I am undone by special effect. Sometimes I fail on the first take.
    Sometimes
I'm the girl whacked on the head. And sometimes I'm a spiteful
old woman on a bicycle, in collusion with the wind.

Laura Madeline Wiseman & Andrea Blythe

THE RED INSIDE OF GIRLS

Every wolf sings in moonlight for his own pleasure, his own pain.
Every girl carries a basket, wears the hood of red, skips calling
out to woods dappled for adventure, for distracted wandering
in the lie of grandmother's house—her hunger, the good girl's chore.

Every girl carries a basket, wears the hood of red, skips, calling
out songs only meant to be heard by the quiet of shadows
turning the lie of grandmother's house, hunger, a girl's chore
to feed the elderly turned into a kind of seeing, how flesh rots with age

and bodies creak ancient songs heard in the house's quiet shadows.
Every girl hums her own lithe youth and becomes the wolf
feeding on the elderly, seeing with large eyes how flesh rots with age,
how the wolf opens the door, eats what rots first, swallows what

hums inside every girl, lithe with youth as she becomes the wolf.
The hunger of girls is hidden under capes and knee-length skirts as
the wolf opens the door, comely and large. He eats first what she
carries in her basket, the sweet rolls and apple cakes made

with the hunger of girls hidden under capes and knee-length skirts.
Then, they taste more, the heady fur, the pink girl flesh
carried against her basket, all sweet rolls and apple cakes, making
the room hot and sweet by devouring. The wolf hungers

for the taste of more, his heady fur sweetening pink girl flesh
as she reties the red cape, gathers her basket, closes the door to
the devouring, the room still hot and sweet. The wolf hungers
and is never sated, already longing for more girl

as she reties the red cape, gathers her basket, closes the door.
Every wolf sings in moonlight for her pleasure and her pain.
They're never sated, already longing for more. Wolves linger,
dappled in the woods of distracted adventure, for girls wandering.

PRETTY HURTS:

Nasty Women Poets on Beauty, The Body & Self-Image

Shirley J. Brewer

SIGNATURE

I've lost a uterus, a gall bladder,
and a man with a mustache
who would have been my husband.
I gave the dress away, sold the ring,
became an evangelist stripper.

Now, I mix salves from secret recipes
at the Rosebud Perfume Company,
founded in 1892. I love old stuff,
even Jell-O, the way
its jewel colors tremble and glow.

Mornings, I dab vanilla extract
on my nipples to jump-start my day.
Sometimes I wink at younger men
from my lavender hearse.
A goddess needs space for accessories.

Angela Decker

HAIR

with thanks to Gwendolyn Brooks

We wanted long straight hair, and we
didn't see our own kinky-headed beauty, real
beauty—thick, electric and so damn cool.
But the TV, *Teen Beat,* even our mothers said we
didn't have good hair. Hair that bounces and behaves, swings left
and right, or flips out of our eyes when we walk to school
laughing with friends and pretending like we
don't care. But when the blondes blow-dry their hair we lurk
long in the locker room, watch each thin strand fly like late-
summer flax, and hate everything thick and brown. We
hate our hair, our friends, our mothers. In the end, we strike
at our own heads—with hot combs, lye, anything that burns us
    straight
so we can stand in the mirror and pretend we are cute, that we
are going places, girls who play tennis with thin
bodies and tight long ponytails, who sip cold gin.
But who are we kidding. Someone puts on a record we
love, maybe Stevie Wonder or their mother's jazz.
We get to business on our hair, burn it like it's June
in hell. Come Monday, we stride the halls and we
toss our hair like a thousand throwing stars in people's faces,
    say you can die
for all we care. But nothing changes. Nothing changes any time soon.

Rachel Eisler

CONK

> *No one can make you feel inferior without your consent.*
>
> —*Eleanor Roosevelt*

Before prison loosed him
from the streets, Malcolm X
wept beneath a recipe
of sliced potatoes, eggs,
and Red Devil lye.
The longer you can stand it
the straighter the conk.

My eyes stung,
but I never smelled the lye
in the pink relaxer Sal
slathered on my scalp.
The boy I burned for
sniffed the straightness.
(He'd ventured my curls
looked pubic), then winced
"What have you done
to yourself?"

Estella Gonzalez

VAGINAS ON THE LOOSE

Good to know that
people are still afraid of
wild vaginas, especially young,
hairy ones. The kind that aren't splayed
open like those sharks, hung from
grappling hooks, fat fisherman
beside them, smiling.

Porno pimps like
them tame—shaved, pinned
opened by manicured fingers
with long, hot pink acrylic
nails. Just like Jesus,
they like them crucified
with a big, hairy cock,
or a dildo nailing them
down.

An old vagina on the loose.
Gray hairs blowing
in the wind, wrinkled lips
roaring. Not as slick
as the young ones
but still toothy, still waiting.

Lying in the sun.
Teeth glowing, roaring, hungry.
They will eat you,
if you
let them.

Grace Gorski

A FAT GIRL'S GUIDE TO LOVING HER BODY

Take up as much space as you can. Remember
your bones contain fragments
of galaxies, and if the universe can stretch
infinitely and without apology, so can you.

Know your skin intimately.
Learn your lumps and bumps and scars
for what they are: the braille autobiography
of your unique life story.

Care for your whole self. You are not
just your creations gone amok. Nor are you
only bruises and goosebumps. Your pleasures
and pains prove your parts make a greater whole.

Never forget who you are,
but never stop searching
for yourself in your hair and nails
and rolls and bones

and core.

Michele Lent Hirsch

BUT HOW CAN YOU NAME
WHAT YOU DON'T HAVE

The man on the train with the
casual boner is reading *The Beautiful and
the Damned.* He reminds me I've never read
that particular book and I've also never had

a boner. What's more important: to read every
novel by F. Scott Fitzgerald or to feel
what this man feels daily, nonchalantly,
this everyday taken-for-granted erection

beneath Adidas exercise pants?
To feel it just once, as a woman, a woman
who isn't saying that her body is
the wrong one but who's always, I mean

always, needed to test that out
herself. Not the Adidas
pants. Just the erection. Not for
sport, but to be certain.

The man sees me glancing at
the spot where he juts out. He
probably mistakes the way
that I want it.

Karla Huston

THEORY OF LIPSTICK

> *Coral is far more red than her lips' red.*
>
> —*Shakespeare*

Pot rouge, rouge pot, glosser, lip plumper, bee
stung devil's candy and painted porcelain
Fire and Ice, a vermillion bullet,
dangerous beauty lipstick, carmine death rub, history
of henna. Fact: more men get lip cancer

because they don't wear lipstick or butter
jumble of a luminous palette with brush made
to outlast, last long, kiss off, you ruby busser,
your gilded rosebud bluster is weapon and wine.
QE's blend: cochineal mixed with egg, gum Arabic

and fig milk—alizarin crimson and lead—poison
to men who kiss women wearing lipstick, once illegal
and loathsome—then cherry jellybean licked and smeared,
then balm gloss crayon, a cocktail of the mouth
happy hour lip-o-hito, lip-arita, with pout-fashioned chaser

made from fruit pigment and raspberry cream,
a luxe of shimmer-shine, lipstick glimmer, duo
in satin-lined pouch, Clara Bow glow: city brilliant
and country chick—sparkling, sensual, silks
and sangria stains, those radiant tints and beeswax liberty—

oh, kiss me now, oh, double agents of beauty
slip me essential pencils in various shades
of nude and pearl and suede, oh, bombshell lipstick,
sinner and saint, venom and lotsa sugar, lip sweet,
pucker up gelato: every pink signal is a warning.

BUTOH

The old dancer chews the dandelion greens
she stoops to pick from the field behind the school. The green

leaf is not smoky enough, is bitter tough, but the sun
shines off the black snakes in the low grass, makes a prism

indigo to red, reminds her of menstrual-blood art, and inspires
choreography: a plié crawl, a broken waltz, a butoh. *Look at the dyke*

pulling weeds for her lunch! a cruel boy cries from the chain
link shadows. But she has *chicoria* warm in her white apron's pouch

and black bread oily with salted
anchovies. Her hair grows static in the cold dry afternoon,

electric like Santa Lucia's crown. She'll stroke it down
smooth with her bone comb, her own spit and palm.

RECIPE FOR AN INDIAN

How much Indian are you? All of it,
red velvet proofs deep in my solar plexus.
Fry bread thighs undercooked, whipped
meringue cheekbone peaks
and a blackened cut of feather
tattoo marinating over childhood
scars, biopsy stitches and mole seasonings
from a life of willing the cake
burning inside to rise, rise, rise.

Erin Murphy

DOES THIS POEM MAKE MY BUTT LOOK BIG?

Maybe these words   are

       too loose

      dimply and jiggling   like cellulite

like my friend's   *hind parts*

       that can't keep

up with her girls' *bird legs*   Maybe

       these words

     need a girdle   some wonder garment

squeezing everything

      in its place   form-fitting   and

    corset-tight as a   quatrain

something invented by   and for

       a man.

Susan Nguyen

ALL THE GOOD WOMEN ARE GONE

Have you ever cried during an interview
because you started talking about your family,
or while serving tables in Virginia
when a man's hand lands on your ass.
Have you ever had your boyfriend
tell you he wanted to go celibate,
which meant no kissing or holding hands,
or ever been pulled over for tailgating
a cop who called you stupid,
to which you agreed.
Have you ever been 9 weeks pregnant,
barely able to pay for your tiny apartment,
and searching for something,
anything, you don't know what,
amidst sites asking
Where are all the good women?
Why do they sin?
They'll take your money and break your heart
and you think *good* but feel sick.
The pill you order
arrives in a yellow envelope.
It looks like it came from someone's basement,
and you cramp for days.
The bleeding never stops, not like on your period.
When you pull down your underwear,
a blood clot falls onto the bathroom floor
of the gas station.
This is when you are driving west
and you ask your phone:
Does coffee make anxiety worse?
What are to-be verbs?

How long will 18 mg of Adderall last?
How to stop yourself from crying?
Answer: distract yourself with pain.
Sink your nails into your thighs.
Slam your hand in a car door.
Slap your jaw with a tightened fist
and laugh at how easy it used to be
to make yourself cry on purpose.
All you had to do was think
about your dog dying someday
and now you think about your dog dying
two years ago and there is nothing.
There is nothing
until you leave the bathroom
and the man behind the counter says
Slow down, child. At least buy yourself
a pretzel melt first.
Then, perhaps, there is something.

Biljana D. Obradović

FOUND HER VULVA

In response to
a peer's sonnet
a student says:
"the vulva
isn't dramatic
enough for me,
but I do
like the repetition.
Good vulva,
showing an escape
to the clutters
of your world.
It really is a love/
hate relationship
with chemistry, as
exemplified
in her vulva."
Do you mean
volta? I respond,
but it's too late.

Alison Pelegrin

BLUE BALLS

With Bumper Nutz for dullies and monster trucks,
who needs fuzzy dice or a dashboard Jesus?
I prefer them life-size with baby names—tenders,
or jewels—something to cradle and protect,
not sandbags dragging from Humvee convoys
in Afghanistan. A gag gift, the new pet rock—
choco balls, bubble gum and lime, red hot
Tabasco balls with popping veins. Camo balls
for four wheelers, and for breast men, awareness
pinkies like cowbells to and fro from tow hitches
in the Walmart parking lot. A desire rises
in me—I want to get crafty, to get dirty
on my knees, on my back, underneath,
just like in high school, but with candle wax
and a glue gun, to spangle them with glitter and sequins
and *voila!* Liberace balls dragging across speed bumps
leaving, instead of skid marks, sparkle in their wake.
I feel so bad for you, Big Boys, hung with twin
Christmas hams—those things look like they hurt.
I used to have a rabbit's foot key chain I rubbed
for luck; now there are Bitty Balls, pocket nutz
swinging from the ignition, their whisper
of a touch against my knee on all my travels.
Is this what it's like to be a man? Is this
what inspired one to raise the question on a T-shirt,
Do you want to ride my fat boys? I'll bet
you say that to all the girls, to the Hooters girls
in gravel tickling your pickup's manly flesh.
Country boy, in blue jeans, straddling the blue balls
chained to your truck—what's wrong with this picture?
Hint hint—it's not *your* package, a sky blue rabbit's foot

bulging through your Wranglers—but the other—
that-which-must-not-be-cock-socked, tucked away on first dates
and church picnics—disco electric, neon hernia,
baby daddy, ball and chain, bluebird of happiness balls.

Kim Roberts

IUDs

Dittrick Medical History Center, Cleveland

Wheels, whisks, wishbones,
silhouette of a tiny pine.

Birds in flight and fiddlehead ferns.
The uterus is a magic place:

dark as a cave, it accommodates
any shape we insert:

circles and snakes, beetles
and bows, fossils and fleurs de lis.

Some are even shaped like a uterus
in miniature, amulets for warding off

miniatures of ourselves. Leaves
of a plastic ginkgo tree unfurl—

no end to our genius, its infinite contours.
On this scaffold we build

a barren language in plastic letters:
expandable O's, flying V's,

X's like antlers, and a range
of two-handled Ts, eager to get to work.

Barbara Schmitz

"WHEN THE BODY IS AS SWEET AS CORN"

—*Bob Hickok*

Corn candy   It is Halloween
Sweet spooky time
The time you can be
somebody else   Someone
you always wanted   Maybe
someone who wanted you
and you were afraid   Turned
away from the kiss   Said
No we will not start this

Maybe you could be them
Be them wanting you
Then you would know
what to do   Open your
vampire arms   Sharpen
your witchy fangs   Be
a wizard   Be a wonder
Don't wonder any longer
Be Wonder Woman
Supergirl   Spider Mama
Weave your web   Cackle
Crackle   Take the one longing
for you into your spindly arms

Rochelle Spencer

YOU'VE KNOWN GIRLS LIKE THIS ALL YOUR LIFE: A COLLECTIVE MEMOIR

Stacia. Danielle. Sonya. Monique, Adria, Shannon, Kim.
Those black middle-class
girls I grew up with here, right here in the South—they did
everything perfectly, didn't they?
Beautiful and talented,
Members of the Honor Society, Presidents of this or that club

You'd see these girls in church on Sundays and Wednesdays,
their hair whipped into
silky flatness from having bobby-pinned
it to their heads
the night before.
If you were lucky enough
to know the right people, you'd see them at house parties
      on Saturdays, looking
cool and impressive
in their ironed jeans
tiny gold hoops—
a nod to the chunkier jewelry Salt 'N Peppa and later TLC
wore in their music videos.

Boys respected them and somehow knew
they were expected to marry them; to this day, I remember sitting
in Mrs. Rogers' fifth grade Language Arts class
in the trailer's mossy humidity,
overhearing Kamau, a confident black boy—
every schoolgirl's crush—whisper to Adria's back
as she bent over her vocabulary worksheet
"my mother said you're the girl I should marry."

Adria's quick and self-assured nod
didn't surprise me then; nor did the fact that fifteen years later
    Kamau actually
did marry her; nor does the fact that today they are still together—
    and quite happy.

You could argue the twin pressures of racism and sexism
    squeezed these girls into
diamonds
That parts of them shimmered, black and glittering.

But I think, more likely, looking back, that what these
girls were doing was rebellion,
rebellion
Blacksouthernwoman style
in the only way possible
that didn't involve drugs, or sex,
or suicide.

TWAT GHAZAL

Lover, tell me what you see down there.
     I tried to look; it's hairy down there.
Jewel of many names—*lotus garden,*
     nappy dugout, muff, yoni, down there.
Long legs, slim hips, but Barbie's missing
     something—just a plastic V down there.
Men's nightmares feature teeth and razor
     blades—a cache of weaponry down there.
Thick books help frustrated women teach
     their men to solve the mystery down there.
If a date cooks dinner, he'll expect
     to dive into the sweet deep sea down there.
Slick magazines are full of vulvas
     and advice: *Don't smell fishy down there.*
Kick him to the curb if he forgets
     your birthday or is lazy down there.
Science says men aren't creeps; nature makes
     them seek variety down there.
Forget my washboard abs and MENSA
     mind. You'll find the best of me down there.
You'll be my true love when you say,
     Alison, I'll spend eternity down there.

MARGINALIA

Because your body is cleft, your genitalia
split into halves like a ripe peach, some lush and
tempting fruit, you must be kept apart, set aside
to protect your value, safe from those
others, those weak and dangerous men who are
inflamed, unable to control themselves,
        their lusts.

It is for your own sake I say this.

Your modesty demands it.
Our family name is at stake, our reputation.
If those men and boys did you some harm,
it was unwitnessed. Your fruit must have
tempted them. They must be sheltered
        from their weakness.

Believe in my words, told to me
by men who have been told by
other men who have read the written words.
They know. They are only
thinking of you.

Put on this scarf, this veil, this robe,
his shroud of sky-blue
that will erase you.
Fade into the background,
without face or voice.
It is for your own good.

Müesser Yeniay

MENSTRUATION *POSTFEMINISMUS*

Silence becomes word
drop by drop

I am a woman, a poet
in this nothingness
that batters my body

the egg that leaves my womb
every month
has a legend
in my body

it has a trace

my womanhood
my Achilles toe

my dog that barks every month

      a man can't be a poet
      a man can be a pen for a poet

WHAT'S LOVE GOT TO DO WITH IT:

Nasty Women Poets on Sex, Love & Lust

Kelli Russell Agodon

WHISKEY-SOUR-OF-THE-NIPPLE WALTZ

Like every forest, I carry a bonfire
    beneath my shirt. And my mattress?
    It's a featherbed of flames.

I'd like to tell you a story about love,
    but it has so many wishbone moments
    you'd break, I promise. You—

you'd end up crying or cowarding,
    or being part of the crocodile-tear
    audience asking for a refund. Like most

lovers, my heartstone is actually heartbutter,
    a heart murmur made of wax and it melts,
    it smolders, the way the moth

isn't suspicious of a lighter
    until it moves too close.
    This is my danger—

I kiss the whalebone without wondering
    what happened to the whale.
    It's inexperience watching

the mercury drip onto my tongue—
    seeing only the beauty of silver,
    not the poison of a perfect teardrop,

like him. Or her. And still.
    Let's not be the part of the drink
    that melts into something weaker.

Like any darling, I trust too much.
  The thermometer has a purpose,
    as the whiskey does, the nipple, the novel.

So let's end the story here. Our shirts off.
  Our drinks filled. Without. Any cherries.
    Without any wildfires in sight.

Tina Barry

THE ALTOS' GARAGE SALE

A widow collects her life,
    and the evidence of her spouse's,
        yet stacks of flannel shirts

remain, sleeves crossed in contemplation,
    wing-tipped shoes curved with the proof
        of feet. From cartons cobwebbed in corners,

I dislodge gravy-stained linens from meals
    forgotten, tangled wind chimes and their melancholy
        song. Cradled among impossibly

narrow T-shirts, jeans paved with patches:
    my vibrator swaddled
        like a mummified baby.

I recognize it, of course.
    Remember the afternoon in the drug store
        where I spied the flesh-toned package,

an image of a woman on its front,
    device to forehead,
        eyes raised to some benevolent god.

I thought I had entombed the vibrator beneath photos
    of old loves. Offered my pre-marital pleasure
        to the eager jaws of a trash room incinerator.

And what pleasure. Each lover exquisite
    now in the tumble of memory: pink and white, olive or cocoa,
        pillow-haired and whisky-tongued.

But, *it* gave pleasure too. The motor's early hour purr,
    a melody to savor later when meetings droned
        and co-workers grated.

For the Altos, I bake buck-a-slice chocolate pudding cake. Pack
    water-blemished sheet music, faux Hermès scarves,
        a bread machine that never met a kitchen.

I consider adding the vibrator, too, but no one would buy
    a used vibrator at a garage sale. Even this one that,
        I discovered this morning, still hums.

DeMisty D. Bellinger

PUSSY WILLOW

This common shrubbery's male form has a "wooly catkin."[1] A catkin is the "flowering spike" "typically downy, pendulous." You prefer fuzzy to woolly but sure, woolly. Catkin roots are Dutch and means something like kitten. Woolly or fuzzy downy pendulous kitten. You know this plant. You see silk flowers or dried flowers or just the male form of this plant in a tall vase, and the plant is erect and pointing ever upward. You take your index finger and thumb of your left hand and absently stroke one of the little white woolly bulbs when talking to someone about anything else but catkin and fuzzy or woolly or kittens and you close your eyes briefly, shudder slightly, feeling a little mischievous as the hairs of this plant tickle the pads of your fingers, and you're still talking about politics or anything else and you grab this maleness of this shrubbery and feel some level of control.

---

[1] All quotes come from the Google definition of "catkin."

Emma Bolden

SUDDEN AS A SET OF CLOUDS

rolling the afternoon into

thunder, I shout savior, slip your holy quick into these queer
bones, marrow me with iron as the absence of

the hero we hoped would cape us, swimming & settling,
sucking up sand with a mouth that tongues

forgive me Jesus, sweet as the baby's fist curled around the rattle
that becomes a mace that becomes

battle, a bruise, abused this body o glory fit around
a spirit America, land of the free for all not banished by

the Bible picked by pages held against the naked of a people
who have bombed their bad girls down & I

became becoming, I at last listened, & below the thrum
of blood & body came a brighter thunder

Emari DiGiorgio

LITTLE BLACK DRESS

Cut above-the-knee with shoulder straps
at least two-fingers thick, scoop neck,
slight cinch at waist, fabric that drapes

I'm not going to blame myself or this
dress, its little floral filigree. Not a cape
to be twirled in a frat house's black light
to rile the bull, to make him want blood.
That animal who gored me is a man,

not some 1600-lb. beast with a banderilla
in his back. This dress is dead. Pull it
over my head and we'll burst into flame.
Instead of a sabre through his ticker, I want

him to eat the evidence with his hands,
a Coney Island dress-eating contest, stuffing
dry strips of cloth in his mouth, or dipping
them in lemonade, which turns pink or brown

from whatever's confined in the fibers. This
isn't a timed competition. Every day, he'll eat
the same dress. Every day, he'll taste me
and what he did to me. Every day, he'll gag

on the tag, the small band of elastic. His one
meal because he wanted it so bad. Meanwhile
in the precinct basement, all of the clothing
locked up as evidence—jogging shorts, flannel

pajamas, cardigans, scrubs—thrash in a circle
pit, unfurling empty sleeves, so much rage
and shame to stomp, to peel from concrete
floor, to hold up to the room's caged light.

Alexis Rhone Fancher

I PREFER PUSSY

a little city-kitty ditty

I prefer pussy, as in cat
as in willow
as in chases a rat
as in raised on a pillow.

I prefer pussy, as in riot
as in foots
as in pussycat doll
as in puss-in-boots.

I prefer pussy, as a twat
it is not, nor
is it a beaver,
a clam or a cleaver.

I prefer pussy to
nookie or gash,
it isn't a box,
or a cave or a slash.

I prefer pussy to snapper
or snatch, far better
than taco or
slit or man-catch.

I prefer pussy, though
rosebud's not bad,
and muffin sounds homey,
and cooch makes me glad.

I prefer pussy, as in whip
as in flower,
as into it you slip—
as in I have the power.

BRASSIERED

The empty Shalimar,
that memorable, magical Emeraude on her dresser,
a tall state of amber, the bottle of Tabu,
from either my aunt dabbed behind each ear
then lower, enough to cover the pulse
before putting on her coat—olive green and nubby,
a gold seahorse brooch affixed
and round mother-of-pearl buttons wafer-sized
that could have come from Saturn.
She buttoned the coat over the black bra,
scalloped cups, a trinity of hooks, taut straps,
its own entity, a meeting of lace and wool,
no silk, no chiffon, no *peau de soie*
or gabardine in between,
with a wink, just like that she would leave late,
a little bit of lace appearing
like the first sight of sunrise
and always as unstoppable.

Mary Florio

A LITTLE DEATH

A man I once knew used to scream
I'm being annihilated every time he came.
I think he thought I was trying to kill him,

but honestly, I'd meant nothing of the kind.
And how could I anyway, cantilevered
over the steering column, contorted,

blind? *Fellatio is honest work*, I told him.
And I'd already swallowed what I killed,
besides.

Gail Hanlon

TRANS PORTRAIT

Below a bruise in the darkening sky
Orlando is a stag in the fog
blushing in black tie
making a departure. Does s/he have proof
of her chastity? Is there any contraband
in her mind? What did s/he collect
as a boy? Why can't s/he fly?

Rochelle Hurt

POEM IN WHICH I PLAY THE WIFE

And yonder all before us lie
Deserts of vast eternity.

—Andrew Marvell

After the honeymoon, we strung my libido up
with twine and hung it over the kitchen sink to dry
next to the rose saved from our first date—
but the libido stayed stubborn-soft and moist.

Next we boiled my libido with tongs, then
bleached it, starched it, and slipped in two collar stays.
I wore it to work with a pencil skirt, a real win.
In time I outgrew it (my husband said he knew it)
and left work after popping too many buttons.

Once the kids came, we put my libido in a jar
with a twig and poked three holes in the lid,
but it made no noise and lay very still
in direct light, so they soon lost interest.

Years later, we found it floating in the pool,
so we fished it out with a six-foot skimmer.
We laid it on the lawn and rubbed it down
with Lysol, then kept it like a quarter
in my car's center console, where it rattled
incessantly, my libido keeping us all up at night.

Tired and tense and feeling rather over it,
we buried my libido in the garden. Underground,
it swelled to twice its normal size and sprouted

up from the earth like a yellow squash,
which deeply embarrassed my husband.
So we peeled it and pared it julienne style,
then finally we ate it with a seared tenderloin.

Melissa Kwasny

THE LESBIAN SOUL

The black soul. The white soul. The brown soul. Soul as screen the film of patriarchy is projected on. Soul as mirror forced to swallow the sperm of others. The poisoned soul. The sick soul. The passive soul. Why do lesbians never smile? Ha, ha. Because they live in apartheid. The hyper-reactive orchid soul. Middle of the night. Middle of one's life. The Middle Ages. How does anyone know? *The common woman is as common as the common crow* soul. What if a woman came onstage without makeup? *The world would split open.* The bastard soul, the soul without a Father. Your skin is a fable. You are all in a sense disabled. Listen, you don't really fear. You aren't really afraid. That dream of hiding upstairs in the village as soldiers shout on bullhorns in the square? You will never go down there. The suicide soul. Soul of the resistance. Let them laugh. You are their blight, but her brightness is your right. *She it is Queen Under the Hill,* the ailing goddess you protect from their sight. *This bridge called my back* that is a field folded. If we drained the testosterone from every infant boy, would we drain violence from the world? The radical separatist soul. Lesbian soul supremacy. In the same way as trees grow over the clearing, in the same way weeds surface in the disturbed, the way a blackened eye will heal once the beating stops. *May I never remember reasons for my spirit's safety* says the fierce soul, though she can't, of course, speak for everyone.

Nuala O'Connor

OH

you shake me out
in our bed that smells
of sea-salt and *cava*
I cover my belly
offer you my back
an unpuckered
body part

your mouth
suckles, pulls,
scooping out
of my fig-flesh
a long, ancient cry
the unseated whoosh
that shakes, rattles, settles

Lynn Schmeidler

MY LUST

cannot be branded. It shoots up the pharmacopoeia
of the jungle's spit. My lust is so powerful it moves

tectonic plates, makes water want to drown. It scavenges
the meat of your fear. So potent is my lust, other lusts

are melted in its fumaroles. The air hangs low in wait.
The sun beats its breast for me. Sometimes the wind is blown off

course by my magnetic force. Around me even the dirt
must be held in place with retaining walls and easement drains.

My lust makes its own rules. My lust is a plant whose roots drink
magma. Sometimes I feel like Frida Kahlo, impaled by

a trolley's metal, drinking tequila waiting for my
bones to reset, planning how to paint you attached to me

by a red vein dripping blood orange juice into my lap.
I have this way of fanning my lust by letting my thoughts

linger like an *amuse bouche* on your tongue. I have this way
of secretly slipping my hands inside your clothes to feel

your body stiffen. I can feel the ocean waves building
in the breath of you. Now my lust is suctioning its cups

to your window, pulling itself up, about to climb in.

Maureen Seaton

WHEN I WAS BI(NARY)

I contrasted nicely with *unary,*
ternary, quarternary, and so on.
In this way, I functioned hypothetically

and trouble-free as a pair of bosons,
which, we know, will happily occupy
one quantum state, unlike two fermions.

Explosive, I fissioned and coded. My
planetary bodies orbited themselves
like a bi-asteroid, a bi-star (blue/white),

binomials, and two cute daughter cells
that grew up opposite each other
and occasionally met in the middle

like lips. Sometimes I was a multiplier
in a two-based number system, enjoying
the way my human fingers desired

nothing more than the gratifying
mathematics of acey-deucey, ac/
dc, options flowing, always showing

off—like a superheroine or a tree.
For fun, I smote the rap of wishy-washy
and plucked the euphoric luck of binary.

Andrea Selch

COUPLETS: BREAKING THE BOYCOTT

Joy works the counter at Chick-fil-A.
She's gracious as all get out; she doesn't know I'm gay.

I'm here for some chicken fingers to dip in honey
Fingers sounds a little dirty; I give her the money.

I shouldn't be here—on more than one level.
"My pleasure," Joy says, making change for this devil.

Elaine Sexton

AMERICAN LESBIANS

Alternate side
of the street parking

kept us watchful
& moving, competing

to park our jalopy,
peacefully,

out of the sun. Today,
when my wife

slid our wheels
into a perfect spot,

steps from our door,
the cross-town bus

exhausted its patience
waiting,

and pressed by
between us

the construction site,
workers smoking

and drinking
containers of fresh

brew, a heaven
we could taste.

And children, just let out
of the French lycée,

recess at last! swarmed
the sidewalks,

what a day!
An Italian baroness

in the Mercedes
SUV, backing up,

from a full block away,
wanting our spot,

hissed: "American
lesbians,"

from her steamed-up seat
when we

would not move,
her car windows

piped down,
exposing her sculpted

hair to the heat
on the street.

She was looking at you,
I think, when she spoke,

or was it me?

Janice D. Soderling

OLD LESBIA REMINISCES OVER JEALOUS LOVERS

Quis nunc te adibit? Cui videberis bella?

—*Catullus 8*

She wonders where they've gone to
those lovers full of blame,
who well knew what they wanted,
though they fumbled for her name;

who stared up at her window,
who sang outside her door,
who came late nights, half-drunken,
where they had come before;

who cursed and raged, unwilling
that she should pick and choose
some other, hotter lover;
that they were last night's news;

whose verse declared time's tailwind
would dry her flowing charms,
while they renewed their pleasure in
some younger beauty's arms;

that she would fade and wither,
a husk, an empty shell.
It's true time passed for her, but time
whizzed by for them as well,

who bounced their small round pebbles
like moonlight off her wall.
Indeed, their loss exceeds her loss.
They cannot come at all.

Pat Valdata

CONTROL

My mother always said I should sit with my
Knees together because girls are not allowed
To have a crotch.

But I perch most unladylike, product of twenty
Years a pilot, controlling my flight path
With innuendo.

Nothing overtly sexual about a joystick, despite
Its name, except the proto-coital flush of
Pleasure it provides,

A steel tube, capped with a rubber hand-grip,
Like a thick black condom. The stick itself
Feels nothing.

All the joy is in my hand: a slight pressure forward,
Aft, side to side; a suggestion, only, of direction
And desire.

Jane Varley

KISS ME

I like kisses. Do you remember
the very first sensation of lips
and the dissolution of boundaries
and the pressing—
pressing internally. The tongue. Let the word
tongue be voluptuous.

Progression, reversal: I want a kiss
containing every kiss of the universe
and then a kiss erasing history,
the only kiss ever, one instance suspended
in time.

A kiss should be a spotlight, a silver hook,
a window thrown open to the breeze.
A kiss draws me into bright light to be seen.
I want to dive inside a kiss
like diving in the sun.

I would like, please, a double sensation
to feel kissing on the outside
and inside at once. I want impossible lips

kissing my impossible possible places.
I want to give myself away in a kiss,
I want to be more myself in a kiss.

I want to invent kissing. Starting right
here, right now, I say a kiss never existed.
Come closer. Let me show you how.

Wendy Videlock

WHAT HUMANS DO:

The candle-lit
after dinner
careful screw,

the under-the-moon
shooby doo
be doo groove,

the from behind,
the sixty-nine,
the is there time,

the I need wine,
the twisted talking
dirty grind,

the Erica Jong
zipless screw,
the I got somethin'

to prove ruse,
the primal bang,
the power game,

the long play,
the itchy-ish, sudden-ish
roll in the hay,

the take me away,
the once a week
married way,

the hail mary,
holy-joe-
I-can't- believe-

my-luck hump,
the side to side
slow pump,

the grudge fuck,
the quick poke,
the hard core,

the tenderest lap
of waves on the shore,
and the gushing, rushing

endless coming
of I've never felt
this way before.

Sarah Brown Weitzman

A POEM SHOULD BE LIKE GREAT SEX

A poem that doesn't plunge right in hard
but takes it slow at first
until it makes you turn over
the page because you can't wait
for what's coming next

A don't-stop-poem
A *pleasssse*-don't-stop poem

A rereading-it-six-times-in-one-night-poem
No, a rereading-it-all-night-long poem
with great closure

Oh yes, baby, closure

A stay-all-night poem
A be-here-in-the-morning poem

An in-your-thoughts-when-you-wake-up-in-the-morning poem
A was-it-good-for-you-too-dear-reader poem

BOYS

I tore them up. I wore them out like clothes.
I ate them, jacked them, smacked them, sacked them.
I furiously fucked one on a water tower downtown.
    I fucked for fame.

I toyed with them. I was a toy alive, a buzzing beehive.
I rode their motorcycles, crashed their dirt bikes. I crashed cars.
I fucked for fun. I fucked dumb. I fucked for love.

Big boys. Sick boys. Little big boys' dicks magic sticks.

I broke boys. I shattered. I held on. I self-repaired. I numb fucked.
I snuck out fucked. I fucked drunk. I fucked myself dumb.
I sucked dicks. I sucked thumbs. I free fucked. I gagged some.

Boys in school. Boys with jobs. Boys with cars.

I fucked them all. I fucked this one's wife. I fucked wild. I saw stars.
I fucked hard. I fucked one who fucking begged me to stop.
    I fucked for jobs.
I fucked high. I passed out fucked. I fucked while friends
    watched me fuck.

I fucked the next town over. I titty fucked. I fucked fists. I fucked
    every night.
I date rape fucked. I sure thing fucked. I fucked up. I was fucked.
I was fucking vicious. I fucked around fucked. I was dead
    fucking alive.

Boys who tried to keep me. Boys who tired of me.

I fucked the wrong boys on the right nights. I fucked twice.
    I fucked for hire.
I fucked and then smoked cigarettes, joints, ate acid. I fucked farms.
I fucked idiots. I fucked dicks, soldiers and the reserve.

I fucked regulars. I fucked myself. I sucked on fags
and stripper tits. I fucked anyone who would fuck.
I machinegun masturbated. I fucked anyone who wasn't my father.
I fucked so I wouldn't fuck my father.

ROAR:

Nasty Women Poets on Bitches with Bad Attitudes

CITY WOMAN

I am the city woman.
I walk with my umbrella
knocking down passersby.
My car swells to squeeze out other cars.
I am the city woman.
I can spit and hit a doorbell three blocks down.
I dance all night in sweaty bars.
I ride subways and buses, and I stare.
I have a laser beam to dissolve men
who yell obscenities.
I am the city woman.
I beat up the landlord every month.
I stare down police.
Cockroaches crumble when I point my finger.
My breasts hold nerve gas.
My elbows shoot flames.
I am the city woman
and my foot is a knife that I hide in my shoe.
My waist is a swivel that pushes off drunks.
I crack skulls like walnuts between my thighs.
At night I weave home between shadows.
I sing and shake out my barbed hair.

Liz Ahl

PLAYING POKER WHILE FEMALE

I raise pre-flop on my good hands—
elementary, by-the-book moves,
and they grumble and fold,
insinuating I've gone too far.

So I back off, patiently slow-play
my overpairs a little, hustle
some chips, and they grumble
and *tsk*, muck their cards,
roll their eyes as if I'm insane.

It's just a table of ten. I'm not here
for friends, but also wouldn't mind
if they didn't all hate me, so
I aim for some zone in the middle—

betting just enough
to milk a little something
for my fairly obvious set of aces,
and my heads-up opponent
looks at me with bleary,
mild accusation, says
I put you on quad sevens,
the way he might say,
but I bought you dinner.

MY PERSONA

I carried my persona
in a brown paper bag. It held
shreds of lint and one hair
that the comb forgot—My persona
has a pecking order. Its first name
rhymes with *self—Always* the last in line.
My persona is filled with
yearning. It shipped off on a garbage
of barge, and landed with a din in
the *Witness Protection Program.*
My persona hid under a shamrock
in DUMBO—My mural penned
by a black gloved hand. It lay chalk flat
on a red brick building,
mixed with saliva, turpentine,
and cheap wine. My persona is not
the marrying kind. Stoked sleek
at the ready in leopard tights,
shaking up a winter snow toy
on a cold and stormy night.
My persona thrives on buyer's
remorse and loss. I bet *you* can't blush
and cry on command! My persona skipped
the needle on a song when
no one was home. It unhooked my bra
in a photo booth in July, then sat numb,
pink nipple held on a teacup rim.
My persona was never a sound sleeper.
A dog barked in the distance
of my persona's longing. Naked
pet rock held my persona behind

the curtains where loneliness
dwells. My persona is filled with
bird song. It carries smiles in a jar,
gets so tired of my persona. Decides
to take matters into its own hands,
holding a pillow down firm over
breathing, until one of us goes still.

Emily Bobo

OUR LADY OF WHEAT

She was just another misunderstood
Plains-woman. You know how it is

with *those* feminists. They wear the hat,
the chaps. They strap on the gun, the bow

and arrow. They learn to ride, to shoot,
to deny their hearts a full womb. They

grow beards to hide their faces—or so
we want to believe. We, Prufrocks,

so afraid of Amazons: "They're called
boobs, Ed."[1] Our Camilla was a new breed

of feminist, a third-wave girl, not one-
breasted, but one-bared. Unmatched

by mortals—wheat-racer, spoils-chaser,
man-killer—we amputate her memory

because we cannot afford her
both beauty and greatness.

1 *Erin Brokovitch*

Susana H. Case

BLEACHED BLONDE WITH SPIKED DOG COLLAR

for Vivienne Westwood

I want the rhetoric. The lyric. The look.
She has them all—her *coupe-sauvage*
cropped hair, tufted. She's an asymmetric
tropical bird, a long way from Tintwistle.
She names the King's Road shop *SEX*,
puffy pink letters, sells punk
bricolage, studs, chicken bones, nipple zips.

Style icon, she pokes a subversive
spoke into the system, sees the link
between *DESTROY* on a T-shirt
and Pinochet's defeat. But her punks
want revolt just printed on the clothes.
Fuck! Fuck! Fuck! Fuck! she insists
when all they do is jump and spit.
Hey—it's the seventies.

We're each a princess from another planet.
I want to stop traffic, too,
in Chelsea, wearing bruise-colored
makeup and a latex negligee.

Barbara Crooker

WOMEN

after Dorianne Laux's "Men"

It's tough being a woman, feeling you're an object to be bought,
an elusive quarry, something to be chased and caught,
when you know you're more than that. So pull me a draught,
Charlie, give me something dark and frothy. Wars have been fought
for less—I came in wondering what a girl's got
to do to get herself noticed? I mean, I'm so hot,
I could melt neon. You want my number? Well, jot
it down, big boy. I won't call you. I have a karaoke slot
at nine p.m.; I'm thinking a Madonna medley will do. Lots
of water under *this* dam. I want to be a player, not a mascot.
I want something bathed in dark chocolate, with a nougat
center. I want a lobster in my steaming pot,
champagne on ice, and two chairs by a wrought
iron table on a terrace in France. Whoever sought
the fountain of youth can forget it. The lies the movies taught?
They're a crock, a foolish dream, a vicious plot.
Life isn't fair, you've got to play your cards, no matter what.
I could have been Dean of Women, a cover girl. An exot-
ic dancer at a go-go bar. Or married to a guy with a yacht.
But I'm not. So pour me another shot of Jack, O Great Zot.

Amy Dryansky

MERIT BADGE

Mine's a stone-gray, scrap-metal rosette
spiked with threepenny nails and a Howdy-Doody smile.
It says, *Most Improved, Congeniality, Goes Down
With the Ship.* Says if you hurt me, I'll laugh. If you hurt me
harder, I'll laugh harder. It says better to curl into a tight ball
beneath the kitchen table than say, *will you look at me,
really look at me?* Will you put down your vacuum cleaner
attachments and your laundry basket and cheap scotch-on-the-rocks,
your Walter Cronkite and pseudo-left politics and your parties
where everybody sings *If I Had A Hammer* way into the night
and in the morning I cruise through the leftover chips and dips
and overturned ashtrays and glasses rimmed with red wine
or lipstick or my father's famous punch; cruise through and survey,
knowing today even my mother gets up late. My merit badge
was to let them sleep. It says *her A's are predictable, she seems
to be popular, she's always out with her friends.* My merit badge
sits on my chest like a leather button on an old army coat. It says
do not remove under penalty of law. It says don't tell, don't tell
if you break something or something breaks you. Don't ask.
Keep your teeth clean. Make it look like an accident. My badge says
she's lost but won't tell you why, found but doesn't know it.
The badge says push here and here and here and breathe. Back up,
try it again. Here and here and here and breathe. Close your eyes.
This time it works. A goldfinch like a piece of the sun flies down
and steals what she thinks is a black seed from my badge.
And I let her. My merit badge says I let her.

Susan J. Erickson

CALL ME A BITCH

This is not in the nature of a dare
but an earnest prayer.

I'm long past being nice girl,
sweetheart,
perennial princess, homecoming queen,
a trophy wife.

It is now my earnest prayer,
as I said before,
to be known as a bitch,
a bad girl,
wild woman,
woman who runs with the wolves,
a virago.

Virago, derived from words like
virtue, virile and virtuosa.
meaning a large, strong, courageous woman.

So, yes, call me a bitch!
Call me every name in the book.

CMarie Fuhrman

LITANY

I got a rattlesnake in me
getting fat on swallowed words.
I got a rattlesnake in me,
it bites the heart that warms it
and numbs it to the teachings of my mother
who said *don't say anything*
unless you got something nice . . .
I got a rattlesnake in me.
Stuns my ability to speak only when
spoken to; I feel its split tongue strum.
I got a rattlesnake in me
whose cool coils circle my spleen
digesting complacency spilled in the pit
of: people-pleasing-no-sense-in-arguing,
(speak in a quiet voice)
do you know who you are talking to?
that is no way for a lady to,
I don't remember asking you,
keep the peace,
pleasant-company-minority-diplomacy
please don't upset anyone
I'm warning you
shhhhh
honey gets more bees—
but I got a rattlesnake in me.
(Can you hear her?)
I got a rattlesnake in me
drinking vinegar, swallowing concessions, whole.
I got a rattlesnake in me, teaching me
how to sense danger,
(handle me carefully).

I got a rattlesnake in me
tired of being held up
proof of domination
tired of losing this venom for protection
every day I remind myself:
I got a rattlesnake in me.
No more to be poked with sticks,
no more to meet the edge of the shovel.
I got her skin in me.
I got a rattlesnake in me.
Just like tall grass, calm rivers,
and fields of wildflowers
beneath this friendly front porch,
(watch where you step).

Emma Goldman-Sherman

TOOLS

Step Catch-up Eye-Strike
Step Catch-up Knee-to-Groin
Step Catch-up Heel-of-Hand-to-Jaw
Step Catch-up Knee-to-Groin

I am dancing forward
For a change
I can back you up
To the edge of the world

If you move down
I go Knee-to-Head
If you take me down
I go Hand-Slap-to-Balls

Shake-N-Bake
Elbow-to-Face
Pivot to load I can
Straight-kick and Side-kick

I can pull you close
For the Ax-kick
I can switch legs
Do it again

You are not padded
All my blows land in your flesh
You are not expecting me to fight
You expect only your own doing

I can flip you out of me
With a hip thrust
Or a Bicycle-kick
I can move through you

Ghostly father of my dreams
Incarnate assholes of my past
Any man who cannot see me
I am a doing too

I am dancing forward
In this dance
I change the dream
With the tools I've learned

How to shout not scream
See warning signs
How to recognize manipu-lies
I can breathe

Reset myself
Protect myself
I can say what I want
I can make myself heard

And if you can't
Adjust I can
Walk away
Or I can dance you

Backwards
To the edge
Of the world
I can show you

I can show you the stars

Allison Joseph

DECLARATION

From now on, I will not answer
        to my name, but only to the title
            Your Feminence,
                an acknowledgment,

finally, of how spectacularly flowdacious
        I am. I am no shineocerous
            clad in gaudy jewelry
                and tight clothes,

no half-dressed woman waiting on you
        in a chestaurant, bringing you
            hope on a plate
                of chicken wings.

Let other women be wedheads,
        obsessing over white lace curtains
            worn as veils,
                fretting over a dress

too useless to wear but for one
        day out of my flabulous life.
            I'd much rather
                you call me

sassenger, woman who rides along
        but does not follow, fellow traveler
            who points out all the curvy signs
                you ignore.

Shirley Geok-lin Lim

ILLEGITIMI NON CARBORUNDUM: DON'T LET THE BASTARDS

In the day's dispirited grinding round
when praise reprises venom, and straight's bent,
don't let the bastards get you (stay strong!) down.

There's one on every corner, every town
waiting for an error, a slip of pen
forced in your daily workplace grinding round
.
You lie low, out of the running, head down.
An ex-lover snarks with a best girlfriend:
that's who the bastards are who put you down.

When the big one rolls and the mortgaged ground
breaks to the world's *schadenfreude,* oh then
begins our every day's dispirited round;

add devil winds gusting sparks at sundown,
torching eucalyptus to furnace, again
the big bastard wild fires will burn you down.

Now hate spills over fences, and its sound—
expletive, silence—to invective lends
in these days' dispirited ugly round—
do not!—don't let its bastards grind you down.

Lisa Mecham

REFRACTION

I'm always in the wrong spot
in line, last in a row of women
pulled to the edge
of the curb to fetch children.
Cars idle, mothers gather
at rolled down windows, poking
heads into mint-conditioned air, whining
about lists of to-do's and brown
ladies who clean, and husbands
strutting around with the starch
of profit, the stench of industry.
Sunlight storms my car, singeing,
reflecting off those other
paint jobs that make black go light
or maybe it's the silver
smirk of their bumpers.
A bell sounds the release
of leotards and pink tights
and the one with knee circles of dirt
raps her knuckles at my window.

Helena Minton

THE PUBLIC BRIDE

Frothed in ivory, what language is she speaking?
She stalks through the park, trailed by a photographer
and attendant in tight magenta, no groom in sight,
giving orders into the phone in her palm.
I think she's looking for a world to rule,
brushing the other brides aside among the willows.
She shows a sense of time, of timing matters.
She gets a leg up on the rail above the swan boats,
her six-inch candy apple heel shines, as she leans back
for the photograph. She out-swans the swans, their hiss.
We wouldn't want to get too close, yet should we
back away or be ready to throw up our hands
when she tosses the bouquet that matches,
the love-lies-bleeding, tear-your-heart-out-red?

Keli Osborn

THE LAST TIME I SHOT A GUN

I was drunk, and the winds coming
across the wheat fields were warm
as whiskey. We started the night
with bad jokes at the Elks Club,
soon wandered by the Pastime,
found our way to The Roundup.
Her revolver was in the truck.

Three miles out of town, we drove
off the highway, into a quiet
waiting all day for blast and light.

Cradling insistent weight in my hands,
I rubbed every smooth millimeter.
Fingering each curve and indentation,
I squinted into beauty. I raised that piece
above the headlights, pulled the trigger—
recoiled, as if a blinking newborn had
looked me in the face for the first time.

Lynn Pattison

YOU PUT ME IN THE DRIVER'S SEAT

I'll haul ass
I'll haul water right out of stone
I'll haul back and launch a rain of blows   ships   bottle rockets
I'll haul the long winding sheet of memory all the way to Judas
I'll haul TV Pentecostals to the booby-hatch
I'll haul reggae to the Arctic Circle and aurora borealis to Jamaica
I'll be the hero bystander hauling the baby,
       the twins, grandma, and the goldfish out of the house-on-fire
I'll haul weeping blubbered love from every heart
       magic tricks out of my underwear
I'll haul us out of this cockamamie
       lame-brained
                slack-jawed
                        movie we're in
this deep doo-doo
                every stickyfuckingwicket
I'll haul the gloat and crow out the silk suits
I'll haul belly laughs and knee-slapping
       HA HAs out of throats
       gob-stuck for years with sour spit
I'll haul grounded whales back into their oceans
       haul the molten throat out of the volcano
I'll haul every last one of us to shelter
       then pull the roof
                over our heads
                —you just put me in that driver's seat.

A FRENCH MOSQUITO DEFENDS ITSELF

It is not easy always to speak with your race,
you of the mountainous body, you do not
always pay attention to such small things as us.
But you should, *mon ami,* you should. We have lived
millions and millions of years, we have been found
preserved in zee amber from a time unthinkably
before yours. And you will not find a way
to exterminate us anytime soon with your stupid
fog blowing trucks and chemicals with zee Latin
names that hurt you more than zey do us.

You speak of us as *biting, attacking* you.
Zeese are all zee wrong words, *mon ami.* It is only
the *female* of our species, such as myself, who drink
your blood. Like your vampire we must have a blood
meal every now and zen, but only to make zee eggs,
zee blood is necessary for zee protein of zee eggs, *oui?*

So we do not *bite,* first of all, we search out zee ones of you
zat smell best—we search for zee most intoxicating aroma,
we land, we enter, we *sip,* we *drink,* we *swill*
but we do not *bite, mon ami.*
                              Sink of us, if you will,
as connoisseurs, and your body, a terroir. We
are searching for zee right vintage, zee good structure
zee good nose, zee long finish, good color, a warm
taste, zee good texture in zee proboscis, zee slight prickle,
ooh la la, I must for a moment.

So you should feel honored when I choose you above
others, it means your blood is like wine to me, with

zee beautiful aroma and bouquet and *moi*, I like
zee blood with a hint of berry and darkness,
zee blood with a taste of La France in it from the past,
and how shall I say, a little bit fat, the way we like
things preserved in zis country.

Your body is like a vineyard with rows and rows of
grapes, your body is the raw material for our eggs,
so *non*, we do not *attack*, monsieur,
we *harvest*, we *feed*, we take what we need to
survive, only a tiny bit, not any more. It is true
that I spread the word when you taste good,
that is why, *mon ami*, you have 55 *bites*,
as you call them, 55 little mountains of objection

from your body, your slow body, I might add,
whose defenses do nothing to us, but
torture you after we are long gone. Where,
I ask you, is the logic in this? We mosquitoes
would not have survived one hundred years
with such a malfunctioning system.

Maybe you can sink of me, too, as a bit
like Jean D'Arc: I rally the troops, I get us all
on the same body, but not to attack, only
to take what is rightfully ours, this blood
our bodies have been built to harvest.
Aren't we a little like you . . . Americans,
you only want to take zee oil, zee minerals,
zee ideas etc. from zee other countries,

and if sometimes you carry by mistake
some hitchhiker, some parasite, somezing,
say, that kills, it's not your fault, you were
born for this.

Tara Taylor

AS A GIRL I WAS TAUGHT TO NOT WANT CAKE

Opening the door the boys wave
to the edge of the bed, hungry,
sweating over rows of cocaine
on picture frame glass.

A voice in my head that's either Nixon or
a cartoon character from the 80's, tells me
this is it, Public Enemy Number One.

Growing up with Nancy Reagan's *Just Say No* campaign,
I knew women with a slogan can start a war
as easily as men. I'd been warned

about Wonder Woman stickers laced with LSD,
cigarettes dipped in embalming fluid, angel dust
that can shimmer anyone into a seizure.

A siren passes by the house. One of the boys
says something about the Doppler effect—the noise
grows lower as it moves farther away. Or is it closer?

A song from Beck's *Mellow Gold* plays on repeat.
He presses the skip/forward arrow on the stereo.
No one notices, no one complains.

The photo on the bed-stand came with
the frame—a girl in a cone-shaped hat
blowing out five candles on a cake,

mother on her left, eyebrows high in fake surprise,
mouth hinged open, a wooden marionette.
The camera flashes, the girl waits for the cake

to stop smoking, lips pursed
to lick lemon frosting, straight off
the waxy paraffin candles.

THE CONFESSIONS OF EULENE

I eat too many Twinkies.

I ask God to make me virtuous, but just not yet.

I pick Tater Tots off other people's plates.

I order 40 large pizzas for the house where my old boyfriend
        lives with that new babe of his, and

I use his credit card number.

I go through my new boyfriend's wallet
        looking for photos of his old girlfriends.

I get most of my ideas off the Internet.

I steal the rest of my ideas from the renegade saints
        with names like Augustine and Aloysius and Simon Stylites
        who spent years standing on pillars in the deserts of Iraq.

I stock my bathroom with toilet tissue swiped from fast-food
    restaurant dispensers.

I swear on Epimenides' perplex—whatever that is.

I take naps anytime, especially when stuck in rush-hour traffic.

I'm a Capricorn with kundalini rising.

I make videos of myself on YouTube
        dressed entirely in marshmallow paste and little pink
        squiggles of birthday cake icing.

In high school, I snuck out with all the punk poets in my homeroom
        and flamingo-ed the vice principal's front yard.

Now, I'm casing the lawn of the college president's McMansion.

I raise my grade-point average like a hot-air balloon.

I tell only lies in my confessions.

YOU DON'T OWN ME:

Nasty Women Poets on Talking Back to Men

Ann Alexander

CLEAN BREAK

After the strife and the cold *stuff you!*
I vacuumed him out of my life
with my Dyson DC07, MK II.

The Dyson's moans drowned out my own
as I watched his motes and beams fly round
the polycarbonate plastic drum.

I sucked the devil in! I seized
the see-thru serpentine flexible hose,
sought him in every corner and crease.

And all the dirty things he said
were caught by the cyclone-action spin,
and filtered out. I wanted him dead.

Dust to dust. Smooth textured, fine.
I emptied him out on the compost heap,
with the half-finished bottle of wine.

Jan Beatty

SHOOTER

I shoot the old man who followed my 11-yr-old body on Smithfield St/because I smiled at him/because it was Xmas / I shoot the man who jacked off/on the bricks of our house / put a ladder to my window when I was 12 / I shoot the professor who said my work was illogical, then used me for publicity when I won an award / the businessman who wanted to talk about my teenage breasts / I'm loading & re-loading / the guy who walked up to me when I was a cashier & asked about my "hole" / I hope you still like me when I say the gynecologist stuck his tongue down my throat when I was 16 / the writer who read his gang rape poem to a room of women students / I'm putting my finger on the problem / the men who pose as feminists / the predators / the rapists / the bullies & thugs among us / my uncle who tried to kiss me when he was drunk / my 60-yr-old neighbor who grabbed me when my parents weren't home / it was my fault / a man named Roy who wouldn't stop when I said no / he said *shut up*, he said *now* / he taught me to love the trigger / I'm shooting the cook who grabbed me from behind in the restaurant kitchen / the famous poet who said there are no great women writers / the boyfriend who left his hand print in black & blue / the men who say we're too serious, prettier when we smile / I'm smiling & shooting /the shrink who tried to lock me up / the boss who gave me a ride home / wanted a blow job / pushed my head down / the poet who said I didn't praise him enough / here's one for you / the restaurant manager who told me to grow a thicker skin & wear a skimpy uniform / because really we have an attitude / we need to lighten up / I shoot all the men I've left off the list, so I don't have to worry my pretty little head about it.

Katie Bickham

TO CHARLES BUKOWSKI, FROM A YOUNG
SOUTHERN GIRL WITH NICE MANNERS

Fuck you, Bukowski, you
brute boxing bastard
with art made from slum scenes
and bottles and your filthy
whores and dive bars

and when you cannot write, you write
poems about fights and soiled clothes and
fish markets and the throes of black passion
with women you left and you
throw a gnarled finger up to the gods in answer
for the earth's grit roughing up your sheets

and you punish the page for being
blank with the same satisfaction
you feel when you land in the ring
across from some pretty pink boy
who's still got all his teeth
and his hair and his heart
with the price tag still on

and you drink something
straight and alone
never lowering yourself
to the indignity of writing exercises
never wondering how your peer review group
will feel about your using the word fuck
in a poem or what your mother will say
when she pops over to borrow

your carpet cleaner and discovers you
with a green wine bottle full of Marlboro butts
and your lip bleeding from a rage and your nails
all gnawed down and your knees aimed apart
hoping the sick sorry world will thrust
something in you to say

Diann Blakely

HISTORY

It's blood, and generals who were the cause,
Shadows we study for school. In Nashville, lines
Of a Civil War battle are marked, our heroes
The losers. Map clutched in one fist, my bike
Wobbling, I've traced assaults and retreats,
Horns blowing when I stopped. The South's hurried
And richer now: its ranch-house Taras display
Gilt-framed ancestors and silver hidden
When the Yankees came, or bought at garage sales.
History is bunk. But who'd refuse that woman
Last night, sashaying toward the bar's exit
In cowboy boots to drawl her proclamation?
"You can write your own epitaph, baby,
I'm outta here—*comprendo?*—I'm history."

Hélène Cardona

REQUIEM FOR A SHARK

Watch out for the fat shark's attacks, all fangs out.
Forgive them father, for they know not what they do.
You don't say.

In my dream, I tread waters with blue sharks,
recognize and respect our boundaries.
I am private like a cat and cover prodigious territories.

Contrary to the bargain struck, I leave unscathed
while you scrape for body bags and coffins
among black adders on the battlefields

of a bankrupt and barbaric country.
Give me spikenard, bergamot and cardamom
to soothe my aches, regulate beta particles,

cardio rhythm, and I'll bounce back.
I'll conjugate myself for you, punctuate every chord,
breathe through the dread, contrive convictions,

pucker my lips to cradle teeth and mouth.
It's cataclysmic, I'm cracked
open, bewildered and brazen.

Die ganze Nacht, folge ich dir.
I drink from the strange architecture of the cup offered.
Wir sind verrückt, aber du weißt es nicht.

When the knife feels like silk against the skin,
you can't tell the blade.
And when you lose your balance, you're over the edge,

the blood is spilled,
you're soaked in it
with no one to clean up the mess.

Stagger through darkness.
Träume ich?
I don't distinguish the dream from the physical.

Kym Cunningham

CANNIBALISM IS THE SINCEREST FORM
OF FLATTERY

You want to look
at my heavy bottom lip
You wish
for a quiver
something to give

I want
to lick fear
from your eyes

You whimper

Call me something
harder & mean it

You say you
cannot look away from
my father's eyes

Look away

I'm too pretty to be
so angry

What do you know
about control

My jaw works words
like colors
flaying skin open

Bobbitt
missed
a step

Let me eat
your organs
smear my womb
with your iron-wrought power

Kendra DeColo & Tyler Mills

WHY WE BROKE UP

Not because he played in a metal band
called Three Day Old Jizz
and I hauled his silver drum kit
across state lines to clubs

where women with bleached hair
and leather vests passed out
across the wet magnolia-leafed tiles
in a puddle of spilled Schlitz

and I still had to pay the cover
to sit through opening acts
like Gerbil Gymnasium or Scissor Fight.
Everyone has a quota.

I paid for studio time with $20
bills, our grocery bags crammed
with Doritos he swallowed
hardly chewed during his Sartorial

highs while reading the fine print
off an eBay Led Zeppelin
record jacket to me slowly
like a poem. *Music, music*

means more than this room,
babe. I knew. I paid for it.
And we'd cross the Delaware
Water Gap twice—there

and back—in my blue car.
And listening to Robert Plant
wail, "If it keeps on rainin'
the levee's gonna break"

on busted Honda speakers
was the closest I came
to the ovum-shatter
and taffied pull of orgasm

imagining his unwashed
leather pants glossed
to his body like spilled
kerosene, smelling

like wet Marlboros
and cow dung hallucinogens
spread on peanut butter toast,
the way desire had its own

ferment, stinging the back
of my throat, carrying the scent
of every woman whose skin
he sank into before throwing

his shadow across our hotel
room, humming like a man
who doesn't know what lurks
inside his body, a bad engine

rattling in its pickup while
the driver sings: *Don't it make you
feel bad when you're trying
to find your way home.*

Lisa DeSiro

A SURVIVOR EXORCISES AN EVIL SPIRIT

Things with him were long since through.
But there was no mistaking who
the hulking creature represented
in my nightmare. First it bent
over me—monstrous, awful—
then it shrank, became a skull.
So I shoved it to the floor
and chased it through the bedroom door.
Screaming *Go away! Get out!*
and brandishing a baseball bat,
I bashed and bashed and bashed that head
until the ugly thing was dead.

I woke up scared. But not in pain.
I never dreamt of him again.

Sharon Dolin

UNPAIRING: PROOFREADING MY MARRIAGE

Change *paired* to . . . *despaired.*
Cleaved to . . . *cleaved apart.*
Seen to . . . *ob/scene.*
Trust to . . . *rust.*
Change *Honor* to . . . *Your Honor.*
Lover to . . . *voleur.*
Mattress to . . . *Maîtresse.*
Under his thumb to . . . *Sunder him, numb.*
Martyr to . . . *Mar her.*
Husband to . . . *"Us" banned.*
Weaver to . . . *deceiver.*
We aver to . . . *We abhor.*
Change *Forever* to . . . *For never.*
For better or worse to . . . *Far better, divorce.*
Change *eternal bond* to . . . *infernal fond.*
Change *Adults are us* to . . . *Adulterous.*
Change *domestic bliss* to . . . *Oh what a mess is this!*
What's mine is yours to . . . *What's yours is mine.*
Change *dependable* to . . . *expendable.*
Change *loyal* to . . . *lawyer.*
Change *nuclear family* to . . . *Nuke our family.*
Terra firma to . . . *Error, former.*
Change *ketuba* to . . . *Get a get.*
Domesticity to . . . *duplicity.*
Change *fourth wife* to . . . *Forfeit wife.*
Change *his analyst* to . . . *his anal tryst.*
Change *her pissed* to . . . *herpes.*
Change *dirty laundry* to . . . *tawdry.*
His ethics to . . . *his antics.*
Her ethics to . . . *heretics.*

Love poems to . . . *woe zone.*
Change *woe zone* to . . . *war zone.*
Till death do us part to . . . *Come Death, do your art!*

Lisa Dordal

PLUMBING THE DEPTHS

As he squats by the pedestal of our bathroom sink,
I can see the small metal tab of the plumber's
front-fly zipper, sticking up

like a tiny, totem dick. Like one of those
painted Russian dolls in reverse—
the smallest version, plainly visible,

suggestive of its larger kin. Even the angle,
a perfect match. What every Barbie
was supposed to want in Ken.

And if God is male, then male is God,
which means we come eventually
to the celebrated phallus of the father-god.

"It's not pooling up anymore," I hear the plumber say.
Rarely does a man enter our house
who isn't paid to do so. Electricians, painters—

today a plumber whose name,
I suddenly realize, I never bothered
to find out. But I do know,

that for him, I am "Mrs. Samuels,"
and the husband I don't have is at work,
earning a living for us both.

Annie Finch

BINDING SPELL

He who mocks a woman's mind
Will be ruined by the wind.

He who abuses a woman's body
Mother Earth won't feed nor bury.

He who hurts a woman's heart
Hides where tears and oceans start.

He who wounds a woman's will
Wills his blood a way to spill.

And he who insults a woman's spirit
Sours his mother's womb within it.

Alice Friman

THE POET

He was the right words
in the right order on demand,
the hot blab of the poetry circuit.
So we promised him dinner,
publicity, and a powerful pull
at the punch bowl. We would have
thrown in Italy, rumba lessons, bought
him exclusive, elusive martyr rights
if only he'd come, read his poems
for our little group, disciplined
in nothing but midwest adoration.

He was a Name. What sneer
hadn't he perfected? The arched
eyebrow, the purple scarf, the right
of the rake's progress through
the field of ingénues swaying
before him: children of the corn
facing the blades of the combine.

Over dinner we talked poetry,
influences, whom he read.
His short list of favorites? He
and himself, as if Yeats never
put pen to paper, Shakespeare
wasn't Shakespeare, and poor Keats
never hatched a poorer nightingale.
Frost, Neruda, Rilke—forget it.
"No women?" we said, "Sappho,
Dickinson, Levertov?" He choked
on his fish.

Reader, lest I sound
out of joint, I offer up only
what memory shakes out,
and if memory shakes out bitter,
be assured it remains clear-eyed.

He diddled his fork, wiped
his mouth, then, surveying
the table and not finding what
he was looking for, looked down
as if conferring with his plate:
Where's the woman?

No, not a Barrett to banter
with his Browning—alter ego
and companion—but a gate
of female flesh, swung open, wide
and generous. A paltry wage
for genius, yes, but what can be
expected from volunteer work
done flat on the back and provided?

Sing, O Muse, the cockiness
of the Y chromosome: sole proprietor
of the poetry gene—that itch, that
flea strutting to the podium to be born.

He read from his "work in progress,"
shuffling, dropping papers, attending
diligently to the fuss of his scarf.
And I wish—for art and the poetry
we kept dangled before us, glittery
as the fruit of Tantalus because
we wanted it so bad—I wish
I could rewrite this story, saying

no one nodded off or walked out,
saying the big man's poems were enough
to fly us beyond judgment's orbit
to where the real stars burn. Their work,
more than bright enough to render the least of them
forgivable. I wish I could tell you that.

Marie Harris

GAME

The painter himself was a kind of terrier, all bristly and unkempt about the muzzle. And the terrier's signal trait, gameness, was one he valued above all others; he bemoaned the lack of it among the general populace. This was a world, he often remarked sadly, filled with golden retrievers.

Soon after we met, he painted me. The sitting made me feel beautiful for the first time since the divorce. I wore a dress made of old, thin black velvet that I'd found in a yard sale. I posed in his drafty studio while he held forth on how you had to attack the canvas like a terrier—never afraid of it, never quitting—and the whole time pacing, backing up, slashing at his easel. The finished portrait was spare and elegant.

After I moved in, he painted me often, though as time went on I became a less than willing model. As a result, there exist, on walls of friends and dentists, scores of renderings of a woman reading, her face in shadow.

He had drawbacks as a lifelong companion. He did not believe artists should be distracted by domestic chores or gainful employment. His laundry began to pile up; I washed my own clothes. One day I let fly at him with all the ripening tomatoes on the kitchen windowsills. Another time I demolished a chair.

Even after we parted, he continued to like that in me: the gameness.

OLD

Back when someone young
Might have looked at me

The truck in front says
Lick My Boots You Worm

And I agree. Back when
I didn't mind noise

Though rock concerts always bored me.
Now I know enough to be bored

At appropriate moments, and
There are a few. A woman

Puts her hand over her mouth
When she laughs. Men who believe

Themselves. The guys jackhammering
The carport who say dude.

A friend says many women hang
Onto their looks, *even up to 40.*

I guess there's been a change.
The uglier I get, the better I feel.

The girls at the makeup counters
The ones wearing lip liner

Kids who spit. Skateboard boys
Who say fuck. I look at them

Like they are already dead.

Peggy Landsman

I REMEMBER NORMAN MAILER

SUNY Buffalo, 1972

Norman Norman Norman Mailer
Bellows from the podium
He will give five bucks
To the very first feminist
Who's got the balls, who's got the pluck
To get up from her seat in the audience
And storm the barricade.

One young woman calls his bluff
Marches up and stands before him
Puts her hand out for the cash.
"Pay up," she says, but he ignores her.
Norman Norman Norman Mailer
Promised he'd give, but does not give her
That five-dollar bill.

Norman Norman Norman Mailer
Says, for sitting on his face,
He prefers Pat Nixon
(a gal who knows her place)
To that Germaine Greer.
How he swaggers! How he boasts
He'll "give it" to Gore Vidal, that queer.

"If you give it to Gore like you gave it to me,"
Shouts that same young woman
With her hand out again,
"He's got nothing to fear."
Not even a ten-spot, just a fiver . . .
Norman Norman Norman Mailer
Promises to give, but fails to deliver.

BUMMING A CIGARETTE

I pretend to read as if the words on the page (Carl Andre's Cuts) are more important than the voices in my husband's studio. I hear one of his fellow students—a girl with shiny otter hair all spun around—ask him for a cigarette, when the girl could have asked others, those sitting beside me, making letters out of smoke. Not a smoker myself, I can't read the curlicues before they dissolve, don't know their language, their languid gauge. *A girl reached him, her hipbones were sharp* . . . that is how their story is going to begin. He rips open the cellophane on a new pack, peels it off like the shirt over his head, the jeans on his legs, and inserts a cigarette in the crook of the girl's fingers. They align and produce a current. They're glowing, the two of them, they're so attracted. I'm standing on their periphery. They feel me opposing them, trying to poke through. The silver face of a dime sparkles on the floor. High cheekbones and upturned nose look too valuable to leave behind. I think about picking it up before anyone else grabs it. Should spend it, mark the outline on a patch of prairie, set fire to it. Resting my hand on one of the power saws until I see how close to the blade I've placed it, I sashay toward him, pull a cigarette from his pack and snap it in half.

Laura Ruth Loomis

HEX ON MY EX

May the warmest thing in your bed be the thinnest of blankets.
May you need a root canal every year of your life.
May you start holy rolling, speaking in tongues and hollering
    "Thank you Jesus!" in synagogue.
May the computer swallow your doctoral dissertation
    and belch out something that reads like
Howdy Doody on LSD.
May you leave that high-powered job interview
    and discover that your fly is open.
May you be at the top of every telemarketer's list.
May you be turned down as a contestant for *Love Connection.*
May your hairline recede with exceeding speed.
May you dial the first half of my number a thousand times—
knowing that if you ever call,
my woman lover will answer the phone.

Melinda Palacio

YEAR OF THE ROOSTER

A marriage of nine years is a compromise,
but the robin soup, a deal breaker.
Still, after all these years without you,

it's become a favorite joke,
a story to entertain at parties
an ease to mask my discomfort.

You matched my refusal to eat chicken feet
with your disgust for my mom's chorizo; for you
the word conjured rolled-up, chopped-up guts.

People said our kids would be beautiful.
Fate spun a different story the day
your parents tested my mettle.

A family dinner, the round table set for six:
chopsticks, soup bowls, tea cups,
the good porcelain set, not the plastic.

A piping hot bowl of robin soup,
blue skulls bobbing in a broth.
The rest of the meal a soft blur.

How I found the whole dish barbaric!
What's next? Monkey brains from a live monkey,
a catatonic carcass from an Indiana Jones movie?

Your mother said *a round table*, like her red door, *means good luck.*
The only cute babies are Chinese, your father said. You said,
good luck is plenty of crisp bills stuffed in red envelopes.

Our babies would never be Chinese, but a mixture of cultures. A beautiful jumble of Chinese and Mexican never had a chance to be, to exist, to refuse a bowl of hot soup, still life with robin.

BAD MAGIC

It starts out simple, with blindfolds
and sleights of hand. I'll be the girl
you practice on, I'll let you
pull a nest of ravens from my hair
then saw me open on your mother's couch.
I'm very still.
     At the reservoir, when
you strip and handcuff me
for the underwater escape
I won't squirm or make a sound.
         But after a time I tire
of your illusions. I want
real tricks, the kind that hurt, or none at all.
     For your final act you stitch
the raven's feathers to my skin, right through
my favorite sequined dress. You stroke the soft down
beneath the shoulder strap but when my hands
turn to talons you won't let me touch you
in any of the ways you've taught. I bring back
carrion for your breakfast, I preen
and squawk and still you will not have me.
     Fool magician. I was such a good
girl. Now I'll have your heart.
Before the curtain falls and I crest off
I'll pluck it from your chest
like a rabbit from a hat.

Susan Rich

IN PRAISE OF ANGER

It has taken so long to find you,
years of squirreling your shadow
back under the bed. And now,

you are here beside me, head
on the pillow, no longer denied.
I spit, snarl, state my case—

and the roof does not fly off, the cellar
door remains well-hinged. My anger
breaks into prisms, focuses like a starlight

scope on a blue summer night.
Suddenly, I throw the oak tree at you
with ease, flip each ex-lover, the entire

neighborhood—the man next door who shoots
the sunrise, the tree cutter, the cat killer.
I take my anger out of the box and tap it

like a prayer wheel, run its messages along
the rim of the world without regret—
love it like a child's spinning top.

Cinthia Ritchie

I AM NOT YOUR BABY

I am Superwoman, Wonder Woman,
Catwoman, my breasts hungry
inside a low-cut shirt.
"Superheroes have perfect bodies,
it's a prerequisite, like receptionists
with silky voices," you said
or I imagined you said or I wanted you to say,
which is the same difference,
which is what I'm trying to tell you,
which may need interpretation since I'm speaking
in four different languages,
which means I slept with four different men:
The pizza delivery boy,
the neighbor with the ugly dog,
the pierced gas station dude,
and the geek at the computer store who upgraded my hard drive.
There were others too, so many I've stopped counting,
a girl's got to have fun, and what's the point
of having a hole if you're not going to fill it,
so call me what you wish: a whore, a slut, a cunt,
I am all of those but honey,
I am not your baby.

Susan Rothbard

YOUR BITCH

after Ada Limón

I'm learning new ways to be a bitch. There are, of course, the old ways: There's how I correct adults who confuse *fewer* and *less,* and if I weren't such a bitch, I'd explain it here. And there's the bitch I can be when I'm driving alone, changing lanes. There's also the bitch I can be when I'm driving with you, and we get lost. There's the night before a trip bitch who hates to pack. There's insomnia bitch. There's 5:30 on Monday morning bitch and 9:00 at night laundry still in the basket bitch. There's rejection letter bitch and we can't afford it bitch and why can't we afford it bitch. There's silent treatment bitch and behind your back bitch, hot bitch and cold bitch too. There's the bitch who needs a drink and the one who's had too many. Then there's the bitch when you've had too many and I have to drive you home. It's teacher mother sister daughter best friend bitch. It's the bitch who tells the truth and it's also the one who lies. It's the bitch who won't stop barking. It's the bitch who's learning to bite.

195

SCARY-MARY QUITE CONTRARY

In the playground, Mary doesn't behave like other girls.
Jack takes offense at her antinomian deviancy. Extra-
curricularly, Jack and his boys ambush Hairy-Mary, pluck
her bells and cockle her shells, lay waste to her pretty
garden. One boy in a baseball cap
(who suffers from inoperable boredom
and therefore can't control himself)
gets carried away and lights her up.
I'm not scared of you freaks! Contrary-Mary shrieks
as flames surge up her bare, unshaven legs.

(Later the boys' team of lawyers claims no one
could have reasonably foreseen how the girl's
freakish leg hair would act as an accelerant.)

Jack tells himself the bitch asked for it, pretty much—
refused to beg for mercy even though he lusted after
an epiphany. *We can extinguish you if you want!* Jack recalls saying,
swelling with mercy, covering his pretty mouth to mask her stench.
All you gotta do is beg! But Mad-Mary only rolled her eyes in agony
(or bathos . . . Was it bathos?
And then weird shit started to happen.)

In the cafeteria, new girl Husky-Mary—spookily adept
at dodge ball—claims she wants to be a Navy Seal. Jack
and his crew follow her into the girl's bathroom, clapping
their hands together like flippers. But the ghost-slut's
managed to clone itself like Frère Jacques and now
there's a whole bunch of them rubbing their legs together,
chanting something obscene. With a voice as innocuous as
a silver bell, Mayhem-Mary tells them not to be alarmed

as she drags them into a cubicle. *What's the problem, Jack?*
You never seen girls smoking in a bathroom before?
Just before he faints, Jack thinks he hears another voice
—far away and hairy—whispering something
very very very very very
very scary . . .

Linda Ruhle

GLITTER

What will they think of next?
I can now have the cremated remains
of my dearly departed pressed
into a sparkling diamond to wear

around my neck, instead of locked
inside a tightly closed silver pendant,
ashes free floating inside and bumping
up against my chin whenever I lean over.

Perhaps I could get the mantled urns
of my two ex-husbands pressed into a pair
of matching studs to glow from my earlobes
like two hot loving embers.

Why, when my third ex-husband dies I can
have a matching diamond pendant sparkling
around my neck, and I'll try hard to forget
that desperate time he tried to strangle me.

Oh, just picture it! Chuck dazzling in one
lobe and Jack trying to outshine him
in the other, with George hanging near
those breasts he never liked to touch.

No more sorrow or inconvenient graveside
trips, just the delightful task of placing
glittering stones upon my body as I dress
for a date, or my own blind date with eternity.

Oh, you say you like my diamond studs
and wonder how I got them? Well, thanks,
but a lady never tells her age or just how
she acquired her beloved diamonds.

Martha Silano

WOLVES KEEP IN TOUCH BY HOWLING

and I keep in touch
with *you're pissing me off*

you're pushing my buttons
I'm not interested in rescheduling

Listen! Do you hear that?
That's my tongue licking

a laceration, a bloody metacarpal,
a fracture; that's my nasal baritone,

my *UUUUUU* unfurling your foothold.
Wolves keep in touch,

and I with my keen sense
sense extirpation (necrosis

suspected; necrosis likely). I scent;
I fang; I phalange; I from helicopters;

I for sport; I greedy chew my foot off;
I trickster; I snout. Wolves howl

in the smoothest of coats, guard hairs
shining, repelling the sopping.

Hackles raised, tail rigid, I'm fixing my stare
on the adamant, my ears to each leaf

as it falls.

Sue William Silverman

IF THE GIRL CONSIDERS REVENGE

Daily, monthly,
yearly, fever minute
by minute spiking incre-
mentally from the girl's
house to the man's
burning images of a wife
standing blind guard
on her husband's
heart. Nausea rises.
The girl's fingernails—
yellow with rage—ragged
with grief . . . her pulse
erratic, flattening
her spine thin
as hope against
the mattress waiting
for nuclear winter or dengue or
vampire bats tracking
a sky already black as
funereal lace.
Who knows? She
might live forever. Only
her anger
will last longer.

Diane Wakoski

DANCING ON THE GRAVE OF A SON OF A BITCH

for my motorcycle betrayer

God damn it,
at last I am going to dance on your grave,
old man;
        you've stepped on my shadow once too often,
you've been unfaithful to me with other women,
women so cheap and insipid it psychs me out to think I might
ever
be put
in the same category with them;
you've left me alone so often that I might as well have been
a homesteader in Alaska
these past years;
and you've left me, thrown me out of your life
often enough
that I might as well be a newspaper,
differently discarded each day.
Now you're gone for good
and I don't know why
but your leaving actually made me as miserable
as an earthworm with no
earth,
but now I've crawled out of the ground where you stomped me
and I gradually stand taller and taller each
day.
I have learned to sing new songs,
and as I sing,
I'm going to dance on your grave
because you are
        dead
        dead
        dead

under the earth with the rest of the shit,
I'm going to plant deadly nightshade
on your grassy mound
and make sure a hemlock tree starts growing there.
Henbane is too good for you,
but I'll let a bit grow there for good measure
because we want to dance,
we want to sing,
we want to throw this old man
to the wolves,
but they are too beautiful for him, singing in harmony
with each other.
          So some white wolves and I
will sing on your grave, old man
and dance for the joy of your death.
"Is this an angry statement?"
          "No, it is a statement of joy."
"Will the sun shine again?"
          "Yes,

          yes,

          yes,"

          because I'm going to dance dance dance
Duncan's measure, and Pindar's tune,
Lorca's cadence, and Creeley's hum,
Stevens' sirens and Williams' little Morris dance,
oh, the poets will call the tune,
and I will dance, dance, dance
on your grave, grave, grave,
because you're a sonofabitch, a sonofabitch,
and you tried to do me in,
but you cant cant cant.
You were a liar in a way that only I know:
        You ride a broken motorcycle,
        You speak a dead language
        You are a bad plumber,

And you write with an inkless pen.
You were mean to me,
and I've survived,
God damn you,
at last I am going to dance on your grave,
old man,
I'm going to learn every traditional dance,
every measure,
and dance dance dance on your grave
                                        one step

for every time
you done me wrong.

HYMN TO HER:

Nasty Women Poets on Myths & Legends

DIANA BRISTLES

Sister, I am the other girl in your dream
about your classroom or lab or news studio
gone grim. Tonight's lesson or scene

is how the powerful, charismatic man
turns creep. He intends to make you unlearn
yourself. He intends to infect you

with his undead blood. He will reach
for your ankle as you scoot uphill.
He will nip at your collar if you depart

from his script. He wants what he wants,
and he wants you to bleed. Remember:
I am a power belonging to you. Remember,

when you notice you're forgetting
to breathe. I will dog him. I will tree him.
I will smash his predator teeth.

Emily Rose Cole

LEDA LEAVES MANHATTAN

Three days after it happened, I grab a greyhound
going west. All I have: a duffel stuffed with socks, T-shirts,
oil paints, a coffee-stained photo of my mother. A little cash.

I spark Marlboro menthols in the lavatory, spit smoke
into the no-flush toilet. Stench curls and thickens.
Fluorescents buzz overhead. The floor lurches beneath

my feet. Nothing is steady anymore. The door clicks shut;
I slump back to my window seat. I need to be landlocked,
waterless. I have friends in Kansas City. I'll crash

on couches, find some doctor to take care of me,
if it comes to that. I'll pursue a new hobby: take a shotgun
to the edge of a lake and shoot at every shadow of wings.

Julie Cyr

FOR WOMEN WHOM THE GODS LOVE LESS

after Denise Levertov's "For Those Whom the Gods Love Less"

Women whom the gods love less
tread harder on the ground
and create canyons they don't fall into,
but walk a serrated knife cutting jagged edges.
They speak loudly coughing up halos
stuck in their throats.
Seduction, second nature that fits
like a pair of nylons
slipped on at the age of twelve.
Clench down to bite the bullet,
tasting gunpowder,
without breaking a tooth.

Women whom the gods love less
don't attend church on Ash Wednesday,
instead choose their own salvation
and covet their neighbor's husbands—
         or wives.
They sit up in bed at 2 A.M. to smoke a Kool
and laugh at the sin of envy, a discomfort
like an underwire bra.
They pass on the double yellow
and risk the collision of new leather
cracked like a whip.

Women whom the gods love less
speak their own language,
the tongue only women
with henna tattoos understand.

The thesaurus burned years ago.
No reference for words,
money tucked under the mattress.
The bank is full, without levees
or dams to hold in the spring thaw.
Water rushes, an orgasm owned
by no one else.

Nancy C. Harris

APE WOMAN GETS AN OBSCENE PHONE CALL

"DO YOU WANT TO URINATE IN MY MOUTH?"

a voice comes over the phone
stiffening in my hand w/ electric impulse—
& Alexander Bell has a phone
installed in his coffin
in case of premature burial:
no one calls him at 3 A.M.
w/ piss in their mouths.

afterwards APE WOMAN thinks of possible retorts:

"Would you like to defecate on my poems?
Lick jelly off my metaphors?
Chain my similes to the bed
& whip them to blood?"

my lines have better connections
& a blind mute poet
calls in the hungry night
& reads me his poems
which are full of silence
& I ask:

"DO YOU WANT APE WOMAN TO PISS IN YOUR MOUTH?

a menstruum will flow on your tongue
& pop out like a polyp
at whose tip a blue stone rolls

I COULD DO ALL THAT FOR YOU & MORE."

the telephone rings & clicks into silence
it is my mother's voice from the dead
& she says:

"APE WOMAN daughter of
my jungle love
grow your fingernails long
& sharpen them w/ a blue stone
till they are needles
then fix them into your skin
at the top of your scalp
& bring them down
all the way down to your toenails
carefully so when you're done
your nails will be polished
BLOODNIGHT RED & in vogue
You will bleed & pull out your guts
which will be neatly packaged & wrapped
like a Safeway chicken's
then fry your liver
(or if you are clever
I will give you the recipe
for a fine pâté—
pâté de soi gras)
ask your friends over for cocktails
especially the one who phones in the night
& you will find that all your friends
will desert you & talk behind your back
for the 5 o'clock news will say
that APE WOMAN is wanted for ghastly murder
the body of a young girl is found cut up

& neatly packaged & wrapped & stored away
& you will be accused & alone
at the scene of the crime."

OK mother
I will I will
when will you call again?

APE WOMAN'S MOTHER laughs a hag laugh
& her voice cracks & turns male:

"DO YOU WANT TO URINATE IN MY MOUTH?"

OK mother
I will I will

Amy Lee Heinlen

SELF-PORTRAIT AS THE APOSTLE PAUL

Today morning comes in like the Turkish sun. A cut
of light so sharp all else falls to shadow behind me.
With a towel wrapped around my freshly washed hair,
I catch the image of a man in a turban, God shining
through him. In the mirror, I don't have a beard,
but I could grow one if I wished, like an erection, strong
and sharp as the sword of a man of God. No burden
of uterus, of carrying another life inside. I'm liberated
as a head without a body.

Katherine Hoerth

EVE'S DIET ADVICE

I'm tired of commandments—thou shalt not
eat saturated fat. The carbohydrate
is the serpent in the grass. We're taught
that French fries are the enemy incarnate
to the gap between your thighs, a waist,
a butt that occupies no space. To be
an object of desire, you must embrace
eternal emptiness. Go gluten-free,

paleo or vegan. What baloney.
I eat what gives me pleasure, nothing more
or less. I eat what whets the tongue and only
what makes my toes curl back, what I adore,
what makes me dream of paradise, what feeds
the flesh that knows exactly what it needs.

Kate Hovey

JEZEBEL

> *... the dogs shall eat the flesh of Jezebel; and the corpse of Jezebel*
> *shall be as dung upon the face of the field in the territory of Jezreel,*
> *so that none can say, "This is Jezebel."*
>
> —*Elijah prophesying in 2 Kings 9:36-37*

> *In the Bitch Hall of Fame, Jezebel has a room*
> *all her own room—nay, an entire wing.*
>
> —*Tom Robbins*

Cursed Teenage Princess Bride
of Tyre; five thousand years,
is that how long it seems?

Now: Bette Davis-eyed Hollywood hussy.
Then *(CINÉMA VÉRITÉ PITCH):*

Forced from your famous city
by the sea to marry sight unseen
some old battle-scarred desert warlord
stinking of horses and bloodied dust—

traded like a horse, skittish pawn
of kings, scapegoat of fractious,
hidebound tribes and two wandering
feral-eyed radicals, both claiming
to hear the only true god's voice—
Elijah, who first cursed you,
Elisha, who followed through.

One murdered son later,
the House of Ahab betrayed—
oh yes, you painted your face that day.
Black kohl eyes, coraled lips,
dusting of white lead powder:
your brave, defiant act or
the mark of an arrogant queen?

INT POV: You sit erect,
framed in the balcony window,
heart stamping in your chest,
holding steady in your mind's eye
Asherah seated between two pillars,
Tyre's goddess of heaven a pillar
herself—isn't she in your thoughts
as your eunuchs throw you down
and horses trample the last
breath from you?

SMASH CUT to EXT POV:
Those finely hennaed hands
palms up in the savaged street
as if waiting for a different
fate to be read in them,
time sifting through the delicate,
bleached bones of your fingers—
one of the few parts Elijah's
wild dogs won't devour.

Elizabeth Johnston

DELILAH SCORNED

He calls to say he gave me up for Lent—
but being as I am, no believer
and not inclined to sacrifice,
I defy his God.

This makes him unhappy.

Now we're fighting—
he with me,
me with his Church.
I intend to convert him
to the nihilism of my love.
He intends to sentence me to Life-
time movies.
We shall see whose spirit is stronger—
a throwing of staffs,
a measuring of snakes.
I am not afraid.
I know what forty days in the desert can do to a man,
thirst, like a trumpet, crumbling Jericho's walls.
He'll come and I'll be waiting
in the shade of my tent,
> goblet in one hand,
> scissors in the other.

Marilyn Kallet

DETACHED

Pele's sister Kapo possessed a detachable vagina,
unlike us. We can't distract
wild boars by flinging decoys. In high school, though,
I dated a guy with ADD, bristles, and pig eyes.

Unlike ours, Kapo's twat was detachable.
She could fling it like a Frisbee. Kamapua'a, the pig-eyed god,
never caught on. I dated a guy like that, dumb, bristles
on his back. One day he was buying me a charm bracelet,

the next, snorting, boring, pig-eyed and dirty.
I'm not saying he was a gigantic eight-eyed hog like
Kamapua'a, but those black bristles down his back,
mood-swings and his rooting around my pants, marked him.

At South Side High, boys grunted like wild boars.
Lucky Kapo! Unlike us, she possessed a detachable vagina.

Rosalie Morales Kearns

THE FOOL

> The Fool hath said in his heart, there is no God.
>
> —Psalm 14:1

Start the Tarot deck with me.
I stand for zero,
hold nothing,
contain all.

I march to cliff's edge
with a whistle and a grin,
enrage the Psalmist, later the monks
in their chilly scriptoria.

I have said in my heart,
there is no God.
Who but a fool would say such a thing?

But I said it in my heart,
and who can argue with the heart?

Kneel and pray, they scolded,
and I tried. I tried.
Schoolgirl in plaid jumper and scuffed shoes,
head full of fairy tales,
I sent words out *there*
and heard only silence.

I joked about hell
and the nuns glared.
Foolish girl, toying with the mystery.

Shuffle the deck.
Pick a card.
Who can argue with the heart?

Sarah Key

THE GIRL WITH A PEARL EARRING

Yo Johannes, your tronie hangin' in the hood!

She in da house, she hangin' fine
She so hottie, lil' chica with a perla,

lookin' mad swoony like my homey Jersey Donna,
your Mona Lisa of Neverneverlands, her lookin'-glass eyes

Scar Jo turned tarty, arm-candy smartie,
Banksy made her hum bangin' walls in blue,

Girl with a Pierced Eardrum, screamin' eargasm
from a mellow-yellow gauge, a mega-hexagon alarm.

Bristol boys' club muggin' town council's money hoes,
street art fakin' your flava, got over 400K pound dinero.

Boyz say you cheatin', packin' mirror pieces
on your camera obscura, make her floatin'

like the fuzz, in and out, way some folk be, here but nada.
Love her do-rag, blue's so gangsta, Turk's turban make her
pranksta.

Yo Johannes, take a selfie with tronie girl!

Your dada teach you how to drape that caffa?
Her neck so high, swimmin' like a swami swan on

black seas, tho black is bitchin', you had her back
greener, grindin' indigo with weld, mixin' it up with lil' linseed.

You colla her white, slash her neckwear, spread the lead impasto
peek-a-boo her underwear, no holla back! Player, you make her

fake it, you wangsta! We know you have no phattie swag,
bling it on varnishin' some nice-ass piece a glass.

Yo Johannes, make us some tronie pearl!

Suck us void in her ovoids, Bach hops harpsichord,
no way to avoid her faux pear-pearlie:

vanity, virginity, so soft, so smooth,
strokin' it, take it to infinity.

Robin Kirk

IMPERATOR FURIOSA POSTS A STATUS UPDATE

She does this with her flesh hand.
The metal fingers are clumsy,

better for clamping a gunstock or
excavating raw eyes. But the task is words so

delicately, she types. "There are no safe places any more."
She pauses. Won't this frighten her friends,

looking for solace? Her mother, already weakened?
Her contacts, whoever they are, as they madly grasp

at false hopes, fantasies, improbabilities, fairy tales?
She nods. "We are in the fairy tale," she writes.

"It's just not the nice one." It's the tale with
wolves and demons, poisoned lands, interesting

deaths. But is that what you want to read over
morning coffee? She erases (click click click).

"Just writing to say we'll all be fine."
She rises, she looks. She hits return.

Jessica Lee

JUST SO

a found poem from The Donna Reed Show

"And to think if I hadn't run out of sugar
and olive oil I never would have got the chance
to be a Joan of Arc. Earlier the vacuum
kept chanting *housewife, housewife, house
wife*. Electric brute. Then at the grocery store
women kept saying *I'm just
a housewife, I'm just a housewife*
which sounds like wet sand dropping
on wet sand. The interviewer in the corner
full of cans made a basic cake joke, asked
if I advise standing on your head
to bake an upside down cake.
I'd like to throw him
in the oven at 350 and do away
with timers. Instead I smiled Velveeta,
said we housewives do the heavy lifting.
I wasn't scrapping—just expressing
an opinion. These days those count
as facts. My husband says 'housewife'
is just another word. *Chair, mule,
housewife, stool.* I know they're never personal,
just blunt. Still, sand was once hard stone.
I didn't want to start a revolution—I'd just
prefer not to be walked upon so."

Lynn Levin

MISS PLASTIQUE

Because it should be handled
with care and can explode
at any moment, it is like me.
Picture a gob of it molded
into the Three Graces—
Shock, Orgasm, and Wrath.

Watching *The Man from U.N.C.L.E.*
I thrilled to see Illya Kuryakin
pack plastique into a keyhole
then coolly turn as it blew
open a door. Imagine!
Something that looks like dough

can kill you. I love the stuff
with a self-love
I never knew I had.
More than my stiletto
heels, Garbo hat, or lipsticks.
I want to wrap some up like bubble gum
and give it to my enemy:
Here. Take me into your mouth. Taste me.

Ellaraine Lockie

IN THE BEGINNING THERE WAS

A woman who bit into the forbidden apple
Call it sin or weakness, stupidity, naivety
Or maybe call it clairvoyance
How all it took was one look
into the crystal ball of a serpent's eye
To see Rome fall with its cultivated apple orchards
and vessels of cider still standing
Medieval monks using them for centuries of medicines

She saw the words in an Old English rhyme book
To eat an apple going to bed
Will make the doctor beg his bread
Saw Shakespeare savoring a roasted apple
with a saucerful of caraway
Johnny Appleseed walking barefoot
to deposit the seeds of his passion
across the American wilderness

She could almost smell the sweet scent of goodness
in the trees' virgin white blossoms
Almost taste the candy-like fruits
studded with cinnamon and cloves
that wives floated in wassail bowls and apple pies
And she rolled the delicious lyric beauty of their names
off her tongue—Roxbury Russet, Cornish Gilliflower, Ambrosia
Aurora Golden Gala, Pink Pearl, Pitmaston Pineapple
And later words like polyphenol and antioxidant
How her body would have worshipped them

She lived the future like a past
Wrapped her arms around the millenniums
of daughters and granddaughters
And laid her explosive bite on the altar of womankind
As harbinger for the Joans of Arc, Sacagaweas
Susan Anthonys, Harriet Tubmans, Eleanor Roosevelts
and all the others who have dared and will dare to defy
those who inherited the Eve gene
Because in the beginning there was rebellion

Jennie Malboeuf

ORIGINAL MEAL

It was an unfair game, temptation.
Eden sowed tight with juicy foods;
each redder than the tips
of the heavy branch just before.
And how tricky to be told
that biting could lead to knowing
and that knowing all could kill you.
With only two people, such hearsay.
What was it He said? *Mali.* Possession.
Adam's throat blocked by apple, bread
of life, the flesh of his own children,
yet to be born:
unable to denounce, unable to swallow.
Lips, teeth, tongue, neck, body, body, body.
One aware that one fruit will end them.
The second thinking she'd found a way.

RESOLUTION

> *Then his wife said to him . . . "Curse God and die"*
>
> —*Job, Chapter 2:9*

"As if!" she griped and plopped down on her bed.
She motioned God to sit. "Delete that verse.
I'll not be typed a heretic reduced
to 'just Job's wife.'" She slapped the draft across
His knees and watched Him squirm. "And where were *You*
when Job tore off his clothes and cut his hair?
Where were *You* when those annoying fools spat
platitudes? Who cleaned his sores? Stood by . . .'"

He tuned her out and stretched His legs. He knew
the script was good. That Satan character?
What testy arrogance to think he'd won!
And those accusing friends who spar with Job?
What soaring metaphors! The final scene's
contrived, of course. That's how I save the day:
Arrive at curtain-fall. Restore twice-fold
the hero's fame. And come off . . . well . . . as God.

" . . . They were my children, too. My oxen, sheep,
and household, too. You dare to leave me out?"
He caught her in a breath and sighed. "Look here.
Who cares about the who-did-what-with-whom?"
He rifled through His script. "It's all about
attempts to learn the why of what I do.
What's a twist of facts when truth rings true?
High concept poetry! It's My best work.'"

Her eyes froze His. "Who cares about your verse!
Green light my part. What's mine is mine." He grabbed
the text and rose through musty air. "How about,"
He pitched, "a sequel? Your point of view.
Take center stage. We'll add a child or two . . ."
She caught His ploy and tossed it back. "How's this?"
she grabbed the manuscript beneath her quilt.
"I wrote my own. The final draft. My turn."

LIEBEGOTT

The hell it is, a hell I said,
a monster swamped in plastic bags,
and on the shore, the waves of dead.

Look hot on me and turn me red.
Untie my clothes, or rather rags,
the hell it is, a hell I said.

Oh god of ocean, god of bed,
strike it down and fold the flags,
and on the shore, the waves of dead,

wash them to sleep and bring instead
her puckered lips, not devils' crags,
the hell it is, a hell I said.

A knot pulls harder on a thread,
a taut-held line, and still it sags,
and on the shore, the waves of dead.

Remove the nightmares and the dread,
I'll fuck my love till loving gags
the hell it is, a hell I said,
and on the shore, the waves of dead.

Nicole Miyashiro

THE AFTERMATH

for The Act of Judith, 1979-1980,
narrative painting by Jerome Witkin

She pierces with her eyes,
mouth unmoved, as you squirm
and beg
and say
sorry!
Sorry for wearing that mask
to trick you,
you tell her. She grips
the gory mask in a fist, it was only a joke,
you say, and you ask,
isn't it time
you release me now? Though,
you know it will be a painful walk,
a runny mess of a walk
but you would do it
You would stumble out
clutching your neck, crawl
if you had to.
You look up
to the black window cover
with its holes punched out like stars
but the slash in it
flashes daylight, and she still
says
nothing—
holding your artificial face
in her fist,
the heel of her other hand leaning back

on the handle of her relaxed
weapon, and there is light
in that, too—
a sharp, blue-white sky
reflecting off its metal,
but there is no light
in her eyes. Just blood,
smeared red
past her knuckle, and of course
it is too late.
She has already
swiped the blade clean.

Alicia Suskin Ostriker

THE SHAPES OF THE GODDESS

when her hands cup her breasts
she enjoys her sweet strength
sap ascends the oak

dancing she causes
the young to dance
and to kiss

she may carry a weapon
a knife a gun a razor
she may wear a belt of skulls

contend for truth to the death she says
and I will fight for you

when she discharges her anger in laughter
white lightning illuminates the horizon
from pole to pole

often she lays her hand over her eyes
like a secretary leaving
an office building at evening

cradling that infant boy
sitting him on her lap
smoothing the folds of her dress: this means pity

arms crossed: this signifies judgment

HANDMAIDEN

I see it but don't believe it.
This bloodletting, this certain cruelty
Disguised as self-expression,
As freedom of speech, of liberty, the pursuit,
Undaunted by the blood, the split flesh, the screams.
You live in your self-sphere, and pretend
It encompasses us all, pretend that you love
And mean well when you are just mean.
Flat out cruel and thoughtless.
Ha, thought I was blind to it?
No, merely trying to be a good handmaiden,
A good spiritual daughter who abides her Father's
Will and loves, despite, forgives relentlessly, stands
Strong, walks tall on the path despite
Your narrowmindedness, your I-am-greater-than-
Thou attitude that you pretend does not exist. Ha.
But even good handmaidens know
When the demon has control. Good handmaidens
Know when to throw in the towel
And run like hell to the next village.

Melanie Reitzel

OUR FROSTY MOON GODDESS EXCLUSIVE: SELENE SPEAKS OUT IN *SALON*

Well, it's not as if we keep score all year—
I mean, sure, my sister Eos has done more men
but perky-winged Miss Dawn has the advantage
of the sun.
                    You try sneaking into caves after midnight,
searching out sleeping shepherds—no available light
in there except for my torch, and if I'm not careful,
instead of slipping under the robes with some buffed up
hunk of moon-candy, I find some gnarly guy
with lice in his beard and the breath of a dying ram.
I'm not into adding to the chalk marks on my chariot
with lays like that.
                    I got lucky with Endymion, you know?
More than a fallback guy for when I was in the mood
(which, as we know with me, is pretty often).
I miss him, and that's the truth. Even in his sleep
that man had all the moves.
                    But it's hell being so fertile—
fifty-plus pregnancies and motherhood will slow
a gal down. Oh, and those three little girls I had
with Zeus? Cute, but they're the worst: always nagging
me to come out and play with the herd.

                    By the way, Note to Pan: next time ask.
Did I need dozens of white oxen to take care of?
My address doesn't have to read "Mt. Olympus"
to earn me some respect. What about an upgrade on the cape
or the headdress? Diamonds. Furs.
                    Way more appropriate
if you get lucky enough to fuck a goddess.

Christine Rhein

"ATTACK OF THE 50 FOOT WOMAN"

Allied Artists Pictures, 1958

I'm eating an apple and watching the ho-hum horror
of a two-timing husband, Harry, wanting his rich wife,

Nancy, locked up in a sanitarium, far from the fifty
million bucks sparkling in his cocktail, in his Honey's

bedroom eyes. And though Nancy's mad all right—
fuming—her pedal to the metal, it seems she's stuck

clinging to the curves of Route 66, the California desert
in ever-changing midnight hues. The apple sours

as I consider the men who grew up on movies
like this one, pundits and politicians sounding alarms

in Washington today because a woman is fighting—
oh, the terror!—for low-cost birth control. As teenagers

at the show, they might have seen the spaceship
as a cue to edge closer to their dates, its shadow

falling over everything as it hovers now, in the middle
of the road, while a giant alien-man emerges

in all his transparency, his projected arm reaching down,
and down some more, plucking Nancy's diamond,

scratching her throat. But the wounds aren't enough
to prove her sanity, and her anger can't change

the doctor insisting on sedation. My teeth hit the core
as Harry tiptoes toward the bed with a deadly syringe—

that is, until he sees her arm, Nancy's hand gone
mammoth in papier maché, badly exaggerated fingers

suggesting a 100-foot woman, but no one is worried
about proportions, what with the shattered ceiling

and all the noises of a giantess waking, breaking free
of her chains, busting out of the house for a brazen

walk toward town, her clothes magically expanded
and shrunken into a kind of cavewoman bikini,

people running and shouting, *Look out! She's loose!*
Nancy must have really been a knockout at a drive-in—

her moves amplified that much more—her hand
a bulldozer inside Tony's Bar, scooping up a tiny

squirming Harry, dangling him in the strange
glow of an open field, power lines swaying,

transformer gleaming. And there's no stopping
the whole town from shrieking at a female

monster incapable of being the little woman,
of looking the other way as she repels every one

of the sheriff's bullets, Harry flailing inside her fist,
above her cleavage. Amazing, how the drama stretches

on and on—remains of the apple long since trashed,
and those congressmen just starting to stage

their hearing—when electric sparks set off an explosion,
Nancy taking a backwards fall, succumbing to the roar

of trumpets, clash of cymbals, and, even as the credits roll,
everyone keeps gawking, shaking their heads

at a bare hint of leg, as if it's still too scary to see
the whole character, the bigger picture beyond.

Alida Rol

WOMEN WHO CALL THEMSELVES WHITE:
A BRIEF HISTORY IN SIX-WORD STORIES

Adam's rib. Eve. The human race.
Names appropriated: Sappho. Cleopatra. Joan. Victoria.
Men conquer. Women breed, knead bread.
Revolutions. Wars. Suffering. Suffrage. Tabula rasa.
Education. Contraception. Mimic. Climb. Buy. Sell.
Rise. Arrive. Crack the glass ceiling.
Jim Crow. Native lands. Never mind.
Hurricanes. Floods. Glaciers retreat. Sweep. Swim.
Limn the past. Elect. Rejoice. Ensconce.
Reap fruits while others labor. Savor.
Flames. Break glass. Pull alarm. Poof.

Judith Skillman

GAIA

Buried here, her shoulder broken
as soon as it shook free.
A birch tree dropped emblems,
symbols torn from bark.
The dead and living
became strange to one another.
I was just a woman
out walking in early spring.
Scents of earth and smoke
combed the air and my pain
became a miracle,
like birdsong
or cut skin healing.
She was only a giantess
escaping an underground chamber
but how huge she was,
and I admired the wealth of her anger.

Katherine Barrett Swett

DON GIOVANNI

I've reached the age when finally I'm sure
that I could take the Don for a quick ride,
a menopausal female body tour
of every wrinkle out and some inside.

I've finally put my Mad Elvira down,
at what steep cost no man will ever know,
but Don Giovanni knows his way around
the body and I'm ready for a go.

Pure lust at my ripe age, one night in bed,
and in the morning little or nothing said,
put on my clothes without a second thought;
love is something borrowed now, not bought.

And yet to make my pleasure quite complete
I'd want to throw him begging in the street.

Allison Thorpe

JEZEBEL BEHIND THE COSMETICS COUNTER AT MACY'S

A queen reduced to this:
debating the shape of an eyebrow,
weighing the merits of lilac lips
or persimmon frosted nails,
lingering the air with scented lures.

I know something about adornments,
what a strong-willed ambitious woman
needs to survive in the arena of men.
There are others more beautiful,
more wily in the ways of selling,
but the customers come to me.

I nude their mouths for boardrooms,
scarlet the lips for hungry nights,
line the eyes in smudge and smoke,
coat the lids with shadow green envy
like some graceful knowing cat
whose preening tongue
creams the shapely limbs.

A painted woman before my time.
Who knows what I could have achieved
in this world, this age that expects,
even demands, perfection.

I could warn them about the dangers,
the tightrope that drive and desire walk,
but a girl needs coin on the dresser.

So I peddle the wares of passion,
heighten the cultured gaze,
whet this desire for the power,
the feasting of wild dogs.

Alison Townsend

GOSPEL OF JESUS'S WIFE REVEALED TO BE PROBABLE FAKE

But think if this tattered bit of papyrus
the size of a credit card, splashed huge
in a two-page spread in *The Atlantic,* were real.
Hand-lettered, each word in what appears
to be Coptic caps, it looks more like something
stenciled on the side of a burlap feedbag
than a sacred text, gospel that could change
the course of Christian thought.
But who wouldn't want to believe,
the words terse and fragmentary
as if torn from a poem—*my wife she is able
to be my disciple and I am with her in order to—*
for the way they let us enter another realm,
opening the way through the world of men,
neatly as the part in Mary Magdalene's hair.

Which must have seemed a river
as he stared down at her, washing his feet
with salt from her own body, then drying them
with its tangled red gold, the gesture
not abased but tender, so gentle something
in him stirred, lonely in this business
of performing miracles, sick of his role
as the son of God. Think of him, leaning
toward her, placing his hands on her head,
the silk of it drawing him in like a dream
of butter and honey and sun, a whirlpool
that, if we are lucky, swallows us all
at least once or twice in a lifetime.

As for what happened next, who can say.
But she knew something he needed to know
and he knew it. This isn't the story
the Apostles tell, but something deeper, darker,
more human—a story of flesh and bone and blood,
the story of a woman at the foot of the cross,
she who hurried bravely to the tomb at first light—
the one for whom, perhaps, he was really resurrected.

SISTERS ARE DOIN' IT FOR THEMSELVES:

Nasty Women Poets on Sisterhood

Kim Addonizio

TO THE WOMAN CRYING UNCONTROLLABLY
IN THE NEXT STALL

If you ever woke in your dress at 4 A.M. ever
closed your legs to a man you loved opened
them for one you didn't moved against
a pillow in the dark stood miserably on a beach
seaweed clinging to your ankles paid
good money for a bad haircut backed away
from a mirror that wanted to kill you bled
into the back seat for lack of a tampon
if you swam across a river under rain sang
using a dildo for a microphone stayed up
to watch the moon eat the sun entire
ripped out the stitches in your heart
because why not if you think nothing &
no one can / listen I love you joy is coming

Judith Barrington

CAVALCADE, 1974

Arm in arm, five abreast, boots synchronized
in a slow march, the broad beams or sleek keels
of our behinds sway in blue denim as we pause
one second before each step into the shade cast
by the banner that snaps and sways overhead—
canvas stretching taut then collapsing into itself
the red-painted slogan jumbled and mumbling
till the breeze balloons it out again.

Women in navy suits lean from tenth floor offices.
Some mutter and shrug, others call out, their shouts
drowned by drums and chants—*two, four, six, eight,*
megaphones—*what do we want?*, police sirens,
shrill greetings as sidewalk-runners lap
the unwieldy caterpillar with its million legs,
its body hunching and thrusting inch by inch
towards the center of an imagined world.

Any time now, any day now, we'll rise from solid ground
and advance like gorgeous horses, our great hoofs
stamping, slender legs dancing, splayed nostrils
broadcasting frothy, grass-stained memories of the wild.

Margo Berdeshevsky

FOR SISTERS EVERYWHERE,
EVEN ON ST. VALENTINE'S DAY

You're asleep. Dreaming of being a woman who owns her own womanhood. Dreaming of when you were so young a virgin girl and four friends, all virgins, all made a pact—all inserted their forefingers into their vaginas in a repressive country, under a dictatorial sky, so you could be the ones to take it first. So you would be the ones to own it, still.

And still you dream of it. Still dream of how in hills of that land where you were born, fathers gave their daughters to their neighbor men and those men, their daughters in return so that each man would have a virgin to plummet, a sea to conquer. A skin to open wider than any sky.

And how those girls were lifted onto horses before they would be mounted, were led forward on horses, and each wore the bright red hat of virginity. And each father pulled her forward, pulled her on the horse, to be owned. How in the center of the road, the reins exchanged, the girls belonged, each, to another man. You are asleep. And you are dreaming that you are free.

Andi Boyd

WHITE FLAME

The unofficial name of God's right hand sidekick (a woman) is *Sophia*
               she means incantation, insight.   she burns

like the white inside the flame. The reason why a child will go
    in flesh first
to the center and wait to singe. *It won't burn you if you lick your*
    finger first. (wisdom)
She is also called a Ghost.
                 Sophia elbows your rib (a woman)
                 says: I remember a puzzle during
                 yuletide. It was a regular Sir Lancelot
                 full of holes. OH HOLY NIGHT. Get it?
Sophia also has a sense of humor (discernment).

She tries to arrive in the guise of necessity. a sixth time of one
    record spinning round.
The lights finally going out. A whisper that wakes you in the middle
    of your living room
in the dead
of night   (elucidates)

and drags your sorry ass to the window to view Cassiopeia
    hidden behind the belt of Orion. Look at all those galaxies
    that do not find you *so very important.* You take your own hand
    and lead it out of the door for the first time.

Sometimes,
too

She surrounds you with pillows and spins the record for
    the sixteenth time. Etta sings "(Woman)" and you know

at the grasping edge of the slick vinyl that every.
single. second is important. (balance)

> *Sophia* croons along beside you, taking
> the elongated melodies that you cannot
> handle. *You ain't got nothing in your*
> *pockets to keep me alive.*

Sophia looks like your therapist (woman) nodding when you cry,
"Sometimes I spit back, venomous words. Sometimes I hide
     in the closet"
Sophia says: both of those things saved your life.

(discrimination)
She drops buckets of (women) at your doorstep, carrying
     shampoo and croûtons.
You've been complaining sweetheart.
Cracking open the curtains to your pain, *Sophia* exclaims:
     look at all the goodies here! Just waiting to be put to something!
     (experience)(survival)

Julie R. Enszer

OFFICIANT

We struggled with who would marry us—
stand with us before the eyes
of G-d, recite some sacred words,
demonstrate to all gathered
the gravity of this moment.
It could not be a person
of the cloth, our religious affiliations
not oppositional but not congruent.
We decide on a friend—
theatrical, oratorical, powerful—
with the authority to marry us from
his own long-term marriage.

A few years later a friend
asks me to officiate at his wedding.
He admires our marriage.
Then, I learn that Eric,
our officiant, is getting a divorce,
and I want to tell my friend:
No, I cannot marry you,
I know nothing of marriage,
but I cannot because
this is the nature of friendship:
support and celebration,
saying yes more often than no,
and because I reject
superstition—serving as
officiant does not lead necessarily
to divorce—though it did for Eric
and now I fear it will for me.
Then we have dinner with Eric

and his new lover and she is lovely
and I hate her, though I should not,
but there must be some line
I can draw. Say, here, this,
I will not transgress.

Kelly Everding

PITCH

The whites of her eyes shine luminous,
beads dropped in water.
Skirts torn by wind from the prison
of her body, vertical field.
A tail snakes around her ankles,
curls and uncurls,
worries the sores appearing
like stars on her dark legs.
She's a switch.
The variance between, unable
to lock time within her thighs' grip.
She's lost that saddle.
Waves pass through her, glaciers,
migrations of deer, geese, monarchs,
leaving behind vestiges
of alarm and perilous momentum.
Her throat vibrates a note,
startles the wind and rocks hush,
birds drop, shy new moon turns.
She promises the cliff her riches,
the sea her hair, and time her voice.
She thins like snow blown over a road,
but up in a geyser
filling the moon with light,
and the birds rise with her
and your eyes and mine
open now.

Marta Ferguson

REVENGE OF THE NUDES

Classically speaking, nudes signal sex, though
in this transcendent way. We are to gaze
at their fulsome thighs and heavy breasts,
think of fruit trees, birds, bees, propagation,
survival. To that end, their faces—I'm
one of those women always studying their faces,
convey a narrow range of feeling: ecstasy to ennui.
They lie there, or sit or stand. Some for centuries,
at our disposal. Until they don't.

The last century has offered us a new naked.
Not porn, the old naked roughed up
for new media. Picasso naked, de Kooning naked,
still mostly guys looking at girls posing, but
it's not so simple anymore. They're looking back.
In ways that make it clear Titian's models too
had to stretch and shit, step out for a drink,
eat something more than the sumptuous fruit
served up alongside them.

But I'm waiting for the nudes to unionize and strike,
walk off canvases and pedestals the world around.
Think of all the empty doorways, vacant chaise lounges,
muddy canvases and gardens bereft of their decorations.
Think of the influx at art schools and ad agencies. After all,
nudes know the tools used against them. Perhaps some will
go elsewhere: laboratories, factories, cigar-filled lounges.
Even back to their old haunts with new deals in place:
T&A for Equal Pay, Only Naked Painters Need Apply.

Ona Gritz

ROUTE 2

Why is divorce so expensive,
Lynn asks, fiddling with the radio dial.
Because it's worth it, we both say,
laughing louder than we should
with our boys asleep, cheeks pressed
against the vinyl of their car seats.
Soon, I'll have to give mine his dinner,
a bath, read five picture books.
But for now, I watch Lynn throw
her head back to sing with Aretha,
note that yes, forty still looks good
and the traffic moves perfectly to this song.
Billboards flip past like flashcards
then we hit a stretch of unbroken green
as the wind through our open windows
sends my hair every which way
making a gorgeous mess of it.

Andrea L. Hackbarth

THE SUMMER WE WERE THIRSTY

We danced, the fire-red girl & I, on the sun-parched bluff above the Blackfoot swimming hole where children and watchful parents retreated into cool liquid shadows. But she, who has always risen in sparks and I who have always been like cloistered soil—we danced in the July swelter above the Blackfoot. We looked for a sky-born respite more lasting but only the dust levitated and swirled around our drought-stricken skin. Because the breathless air wanted movement because we were thirsty like the rising dust for rain because there might've been something to the feeling that our thighs—soft still, and heavy now—had some power in them after all, we still danced, the fire-red girl & I. Her flame-feet and my dirt-soles pounded rhythms out of sparks and earth and the wind picked up the drought-stricken grasses and made them sing sweet sussing songs above our feet's percussion until the waters of the Blackfoot took notice and gathered themselves into clouds and our girl-thighs—soft and heavy—felt the coming respite, gathered up their mother-strength and gave one last entreaty to the rain. The clouds began to find their way in fat droplets to join our spark-earth rhythms, to speckle then splatter then drench the grey rocks black, to streak patterns into our dust-brown thighs, to permeate the air with scents of growing things, to settle the earth at our feet. We stopped, the fire-red girl & I. We raised our faces to find our sky-born blessing. We turned, descending in silence from the new-quenched bluff above the Blackfoot, unable to find the just-right words for what we'd done, unwilling to say whether we'd done anything at all, uncertain what sort of things we'd found in that rain.

Ashley Mace Havird

THE HARVEST

Mid-afternoon, the porch, and a book: *Wild Trees of the Caymans.*
Hooked through the foot, the conch hangs from the railing.
Susan, adrift on her lounge chair, snores.
Crab Bush, Indian Almond, Pepper Cinnamon, Balsam.
It lifts its shell, lets it drop.

At Greenhouse Reef, spawning silted the water.
Conchs: hundreds. We turned them over to the sun.
I plucked from this sea garden of mouths the one
whose fluted edge, butter-yellow, paled
to pink-white translucence, deepened in its throat to rose.

A local told us how to kill it clean—
no gobbets secreted in whorls to stink and draw ants.
A trolling hook filched from her ex's tackle box—
she offered to do the deed. But I'd brought it this far,
off-season, to the house she'd gotten to keep.

Wild Fig, Ironwood, Bitter Plum, Cherry.
The flesh cringed above the stony operculum.
One jab, a second, and the barb twisted through.
Strung up, the snail lengthened, a rope of taffy,
from the swift weight of its shell.

"I can't believe I'm doing this." I'm sweating.
"You wanted it." Divorce has toughened her.
The sea's iris shimmers around patches of Sargassum weed,
brown-red, scabrous. One stalked eye wavers, seems to *see.*
All day, all night, another morning; the shell falls.

Bull Hoof, Plopnut, poison Manchineel.
Etched with pigment from the vivid shell—
mango, papaya, cream—the mantle hangs.
I balance on coral stumps in ripe tidal pools,
release it to the scavengers, those merciful and quick.

Mary B. Moore

AMANDA AND THE MAN-SOUL

Amanda likes the mandolin's twang
she also likes a good man and has one
inside her, says Jung. Her mantra
is *Amanda, Man, Amanda.*
She lies in the sun tanning
and listens to bluegrass,
but she can't forget about the little man.
She is reading Jung.
She is not who you think she is.
She's just blackened her spiked hair
and bathes herself in aloe
to soothe her fresh tats, her arm cuts.
Not to imply she's unhealthy.

Amanda thinks the man lives in her chest.
She'd like to cut him out, but where would he go?
Tragic face, happy face, sly face, and so forth.
Jung says the man inside is her soul,
the sexes crossed. She's his hidey hole.

Amanda never hides.
The sun's on the book, on her lap, it's hot
in her jet black hair. She'd like
a sturdy girl-soul, thick-knuckled,
chin squared, feet wide from working
the soil. She's nobody's
knock-over. She'd play mandolin
for its moods, both lyric and bold.
But Amanda's stuck with the middle man

who taps in her chest like iambs.

JC Reilly

FAT GIRLS GET GROPED TOO

in public places.

     On a northbound MARTA train,
where I lean on a pole by the door,
a man's hand slips around me

     and cups my breast—
testing its fullness a moment, his finger
teasing for my nipple's response.

     Rigid, a gasp like winter in my throat,
I shrink from him—but there is no space
to step away in the crowded car,

     and I cannot make myself smaller—
The train slows, enters Five Points.
What if I get off at the stop, just to breathe?

     What if he—follows—me?
The voices of a thousand women caution:
Stay here. Stay visible. Stay safe—as you can.

     The doors close. The train pulls away,
picks up speed, and he is too close,
like sulphur and sweat. I tell myself

     Maybe it was an accident—
Maybe he didn't know what he was doing—
Maybe—maybe—I imagined it—

The voices of a thousand women whisper:
You know what you felt. You know what he did.
You mustn't—you can't—react.

The train jolts. He crushes against me.
Panic, metallic, mine, sparks like the third rail.
Breath, feral and chitinous, prickles at my neck.

I know what he's thinking—*you are fat.*
No one would believe you if you say anything.
Nobody wants a fat woman. I can get away with this.

No world is safe, with men like him:
in his eyes, like all women, I've no right
to myself—a thing to be sullied—silenced.

You must not escalate the situation,
the voices of a thousand women urge.
Do nothing. He could kill you.

Four stops later, Midtown.
Passengers throng the doors: his hand clamps
on my breast again. He takes what he wants.

If I do nothing—if I let this shame
twist at me garrote-tight—*if I do nothing*—
I use the train's sudden lurch

to ram my elbow into his chest—
stomp his foot for good measure,
the train's momentum, mine. He grunts

with the impact. I say *Oh sorry,*
didn't mean to bump you! I turn and face
him, the cockroach in a black suit.

He mumbles, *Fuck you fat bitch,*
and scuttles off at Lindbergh. The doors close.
The voices of a thousand women well up,

                                    sing.

Helen Ruggieri

THE LONG WAR

He came back from that war
and the only way you could tell
he'd been away was that
he'd never blink.

He asked Kate out to dinner,
drove behind the stadium
pried her legs apart
told her she owed him, big.

When he was done, she ran
home through the alleys
because she was afraid,
didn't want anyone to know.

We didn't tell her to go
to the cops. We knew better
than that already. So nobody
knew but us and we never told.

He married a girl from our class;
we spit on the sidewalk when they
came out of church, looked at him
hard so he'd know we knew.

Kate got a job in D.C.,
died in a wreck on the beltway.
Her mother had her buried
in Sacred Heart.

We let the air out of his tires
when his car was parked by
the Barracuda or the VFW,
called when he wasn't home

and asked for him in a sexy voice.
New Year's Eve we stole his coat
from the Legion and pissed on it,
threw it in the snow by his car.

At our reunion he sat at the bar
and drank non-stop. We whispered
to his wife so he wouldn't hear,
cut the finish on his car with a fork.

At the next, he didn't come—divorced.
His wife said he'd stay up late
and sometimes she'd hear him cry,
and then, she whispered, he couldn't

get it up. The war, you know.
Just punishment, we thought, relieved.
We would have gone on forever
avenging a ghost of ourselves.

Denise Sedman

NASTY GIRLS FROM DETROIT CITY

We're the nasty girls from Detroit city
Been roasted over the open flame,
Until our butts burn, oh so hot, baby
Boys better get used to chewing tough meat
Because we're not going down for it
We've got the power now,
So keep your pants on

We got Motown in our veins
Vietnam clear in our brains,
Said we're gonna take you down
When midnight comes around

Civil disobedience crossed our door
No time for your right-wing trash
You got that right, baby,
Somethin's gonna change

Been pulled down strand-by-strand
Seen too many made-for-TV movies
With trumped-up bitches on parade
Read 100 Wayne Dyer books
And still ain't got no promotion

It's been too damn long
since we burned our bras
Ain't replaying that tape
Can't turn back to yesterday,
Somethin's gonna change

Used to be when miniskirts
Gave you a beaver shot,
Trapped you in our crotch, N.O.W.
We ain't no gentle rose or nothing,
We're the nasty girls from Detroit City

Christine Stewart-Nuñez

BAD GIRL

Hold up the universe, good girl.

—Molly Peacock

Peel back the universe, bad girl. Wear black minis
and fishnets for us all. Tell that boss
to fuck off. Take blame for the affair.
Leave lovers bleeding in bed for other girls
to save. Spend your whole paycheck on yourself.

Punch through the rules, bad girl. Publish
nude photos of yourself. Stab the rapist to kill.
Shatter ceilings with your stilettos; find
new uses for your bra. Leave Sunday mornings
for the spa and evenings for sipping scotch.

Slice open the law, bad girl. Tattoo
lies across your thighs. Flaunt red
leather at funerals and across Central Park.
Worship women, and don't apologize
for hating kids and kittens—both whine.

Tear down the wall, bad girl. Reveal
cleavage to save a buck at the checkout lane.
Eat Wall Street boys for breakfast; spend dividends
on yourself. Kiss and tell *new* lovers
the details. Bad girls don't love their moms.

Break it up, bad girl. Shake your sweet
ass as you walk. Turn your back to bitches
who can't cope. Everyone wants freedom.
Besides. Those pink-cheeked girls are exhausted.
Don't smile, and they'll take cues from you.

Susan Vespoli

I COME FROM A LINE OF WOMEN

Named after saints, queens,
and mothers of Jesus
who knit pictures into sweaters,
channel Ouija boards into books,
and defecate into cranberry boxes
while on road trips by themselves.

I come from a line of women
who glue false eyelashes
onto their lids in their eighties,
sport jungle pelt prints,
and wallpaper bathrooms
with photos of Tom Jones.

I come from a line of women
who drag children cross country by train
to locate philandering husbands
and say meals must contain a root,
leaf, and seed vegetable.

I come from a line of women
who fly Beechcrafts, lead Girl Scouts,
travel the world and say they will
only come home in a box.

I come from a line of women
who drop dead outside of parked cars
still holding the keys in their hands.

Andrena Zawinski

SOME WOMEN, TAKE HEART

> *. . . I feel the*
> *rage of a soldier standing over the body of*
> *someone sent to the front lines*
> *without training*
> *or a weapon.*
>
> —Sharon Olds, "Indictment of Senior Officers"

Some women learn to take it with a stiff
upper lip, stitched up tight, standing up,
right on the kisser, in the teeth, jaw wired,
bruised cheek swollen on a clip under
the eye. Some women take it flat on
their backs, slapped in a cast, choked,
roped in a free-kill-zone, run down out
on the road, statistics for the *Times.*

Some women take it into the heart-
land, run with what they own, new job, new
home, new name in balled fists, chased across
state lines, life on the line—kicked down, kid-
napped, taken back. Some women breathe in
old dreams, slip under night covers, think
they stink on the sheets, knuckle under
enemy outposts in their minds.

Some women try to make it, fix it, get it
right, can't do anything right—beaten up,
beaten down, beaten to death between thin
walls, windows up. Some women start up
at the door slam, click of the briefcase clasp,

tinkle of ice in the glass, Bourbon splashed
on the floor. Some women can't take any
more morning after sweet talk, panes out—
board it up, change the locks, bar the doors.

Some women—the ball busters, castrators,
man haters—stick out their tongues on a dare,
tear in the skin, go for the muscle and scream:
no more, bloody spit ribboning lips, mouthy
at the firing line like they mean it.
Some women take a match to the gas,
burn the bed, end up rattling chains behind bars.
Some women *want a revolution like a lover* [2]
and a full metal jacket for a heart.

[2] Robin Morgan, "Monster"

Barbara Zimmerman

REQUIEM

When I die bake rhubarb pies, hand out Manhattan perfects,
toss out the
teetotalers,
play Etta James on the stereo, volume on max, mellow the mix
with reggae
and ragtime,
pile up all photos, love letters, and tax returns, then build a bonfire,
roast marshmallows,
the marriage license,
invite my ex, spiking his scotch with saccharin and arsenic,
lie to his lover and tell her I liked her,
then line my coffin with rejects from journals,
bind all my stories with berries and bourbon, read them
then suck the spine dry,
dig for the bong stashed in the shoebox, last row to the right
in the back closet,
tamp it with weed from the coffee can, top shelf of the pantry,
get wacky and wise,
then boogie on down to the dive on the corner, cork all
your comments till
you're drunk and delightful, then pressure the priest to toss back
a toddy,
sing me to heaven and settle all scores.

SHE WORKS HARD FOR THE MONEY:

Nasty Women Poets on Work

Patricia Behrens

PENELOPE AT WORK

She found the urge to weave had gone
that tedious daily making—over/under—
of cloth intended only to be rent apart.

Now she wanted high-piled stones to rise
that her deft hands had wedged to last
so strong that neither wind, nor enemies

nor she could tear apart the edifice of rock
she'd make along the island's eastern shore.
A sailor might sight it if he were staring west.

From the rock-cleared land something might grow.
And he, if he were to come home, would know
not how she'd held back, but what she'd done.

Nola Garrett

THE PASTOR'S WIFE CONSIDERS HER CHOPS

I'm from a long line of butchers, called
to slaughter hogs, steers, dry milk cows
on the haymow side of bank barns
where the animals never go.
                              I prize knives,
various mallets, surprise, spare words.
I saw. I slice. I trim. I discard. I
rearrange body parts. I will grind
anything for the sake of tenderness.

Karen Head

THE OTHER SIDE OF THE TRACKS

What if I chucked it all,
began calling myself Candi,
(with a heart over the "i")
stopped in at Walmart to buy
a jean-skirt, a tank top,
and a can of Aqua Net,
hitchhiked to a small town
just outside Birmingham, AL
taking on a part-time waitress gig,
mornings at the Waffle House,
evenings spent pot-smoking
and fucking anyone who could pay
enough, just to make ends meet,
dealt a little meth near train crossings
from a junker with a hood that would pop up
whenever I gunned the engine or drove over 45,
until the day came when I saw
a Laura Ashley knockoff jumper
hanging out of the Salvation Army bin
and felt the Spirit move me,
took to preaching from the self-serve pumps
at the Shell station that sells trucker porn,
answering to any Biblical name,
believing, like proper church matrons,
that I was somehow more redeemable,
worth a dollar's charity, when before
they couldn't be bothered to leave
me a tip when I served them coffee.

Rage Hezekiah

FULL BELLY FARM

We pile into the Datsun's bed, beneath
the morning California sun. Bouncing
over farm terrain towards the field,
all of us wield freshly sharpened knives.

Thick red and green stripes
of cabbage ribbon the distance.
Knees bent, we begin the collection,
hurling heavy vegetables into bins. The men

are always laughing, a sexual joke
in every action. They hunch
behind each other, feigning penetration.
I'm always laughing too. We pile the boxes high,

pausing to swig water from delicate plastic cups.
Pancho asks, *Raquel, te gustan hombres o mujeres?*
Qué piensas? My reply a question. *What do you think?*
Then he pulls a worm from dark soil, a thick form

wriggling in his fingers, *Cómalo, Raquel! Eat it!*
I tug the writhing thing from him, open wide
as the other men freeze in disbelief. The form bursts
between my teeth as I chew, grainy and bitter,

and I refuse to flinch. Proving I belong
among them, I'm strong enough to stay.

Donna Kaz

WAITRESS

Before I leave I stack up the coffee cups, brush
the crumbs into a neat pile, ball up the napkins,
stuff the sugar packets into place then remember
I'm not a waitress anymore, not faceless anymore,
not one of millions of women in white shirts, black pants,
black shoes, white aprons, serving up phony smiles behind
six cups of coffee stacked to the sky, three small salads
balanced up the arm, side of fries held in place by a pinky,
bottle of ketchup perched against a shoulder, taking a drink order,
a dessert order, an order from the manager and a round
of vulgarities from the "sous" chef, not spending
my two A.M.'s filling half empty salt shakers, adjusting mustard jars
next to crumpled Sweet'n Lows, not giving someone
a few more minutes anymore, not giving until
good and ready to give, waiting
until the last possible second, teetering
on the precipice between twenty percent and squat,
not sassy anymore, proud of the fact that nobody
ever claimed squatters rights in my station, nobody
ever fired me because I quit first, nobody stiffed me
and was not cursed to burn in hell for all time, not armed
with revenge anymore, ready to fill the reservation book
with bogus names, lay down on the salad bar and refuse to move,
barricade myself inside the side station, throw myself
off the steam table, die every night with my apron on.

Rose Kelleher

EVERY GIRL FOR HERSELF

"Not in my house!" my mother shouts. The boys
are playing dodgeball with an orange, walls
shake, floors squeak, doors slam. My Barbie dolls
are headless, thus oblivious to noise.

At 6:01, my father says amen,
and that's the starting gun: we race to dine.
The table's a tangle of longer arms than mine,
but I—ha ha!—am quick, though only ten.

The flashback ends. Cut to a conference table,
where one blouse breaks a ring of polo shirts:
a glasses girl, industrious and able,
the type who argues, not the type who flirts.

An intern comes with donuts. I'm amazed
at my own speed as I snag the chocolate glazed.

Cindy King

MOTHER OF INVENTION

Who first fashioned fishnet stockings,
wearable windows for the high-rise
of the female leg, these panes
that divide thighs into endless peepshows,
elasticated graphs, spanning ankles, knees,
and calves, that chart the unknown like sextants,
in their use of heavenly bodies?

It was neither punk nor prostitute
nor burlesque dancer,
neither derby queen nor stripper.
No cathouse madam or saloon gal,
Vegas waitress or the ones
with satin ears and the bunny tails.

Not the checkout girl, whose legs
do the shop owner's standing,
or the secretary, too busy with her boss'
running around. Nor could it be
the housekeeper, on her feet so much,
she can no longer stand
up for herself.

Some say it was a woman,
mother to nothing but invention.
She lived by the river alone
and wished to fish for both dinner
and compliments at the same time.

Others credit fishermen for their creation,
perhaps on a day when their bare-breasted
figurehead was indifferent to the waves
that threw themselves at her and
nets caught nothing but water.

I'd like to think it was a mermaid
with no use for the hosiery's makeshift scales,
one who defines human females
by what's between their "double-tails,"
sees legs as but a means to move it
from man to man. She knows
too well that a kiss comes
from the same place as a curse,
that we also piss from the place
where we love.

Artifact of unacknowledged ingenuity,
these stockings, whose inventor remains
a mystery, or if nothing else, a painful reminder
of the ocean's glass ceiling.

Juanita Kirton

FEMALE SOLDIER

Boots on the ground
don't look back
hauling my seventy-five-pound pack

Impossible mission to complete
painted toes don't mix with sand
scope out the enemy among us we seek

Married my M-16
left my babies and man behind
improvised mines, child soldiers in between

Eat, sleep, shit with my weapon
covered heads all look the same
beards on faces share no smiles, who shoulders the blame?

The enemy can't be seen
hot sun beating down
duty and mission, we got the high ground

Brothers-in-arms got my back
shattered bodies and lost dreams
unwanted comforts in my sack

Home is nowhere just a click
empty smiles the hidden enemy
mangled limbs, psyche sick

PROMOTION

I sit with hands wrapped
around the steaming mug.
My new office is freezing,
my desk just below the vents
that blow cold
air regardless of the outside
temperature.
I sit and sip
hot water—not tea or coffee,
just water.
Just the mug to warm
my hands and the liquid
to warm my throat.

Only men have inhabited
this space and I knew
it would be cold but
the requirement of layers
and a lined bra seemed
a worthy trade-off
for authority and power.

I celebrate
by ordering business cards
with my new title
printed on them.
Tomorrow I'll wear
an unlined bra.
I'll let my erect
nipples walk into the room
before me—guns blazing.

Ronna Magy

TIES THAT BIND

1971. Dee and I pull up long answering service cords.
Plug them into the board.
Circle Answering Service. May I help you? we say.
A buck seventy-five an hour.
For this we don blue aprons.
Work through the night.
Answer plumbers' electricians' and doctors' phones.
Take messages.
Connect emergency calls.

In the bowels of the Hotel San Diego
where we work downtown,
uniformed sailors slouch in outer doorways.
Hey baby they taunt.
Look us over
up and down.
As we open glass doors.
Walk inside.
Go to work.

Telephone cords stretch 'round our lives.
Dee and I are friends.
Go to movies together.
Giggle about dresses and nails.
Things girls gossip about.
Ways to style our hair.

We plan to room together.
Discuss the apartment where we'll live and
moving in.
Her couch, my kitchen table.

The objects of life.
Colors of the bedroom.
Where we'll each have a bed.
Stretch the connection from her place downtown
to mine in Golden Hill.
A few more miles of telephone wire.

That moment over dinner when I tell her
I'm lesbian.
Cords in her throat tighten.
She stammers.
Can't allow a friend of hers
would be anything other than straight.
Her blue eyes, sprayed hair, polished nails
still in place.
Stripes down her blue dress twisting
just a bit more
to the right.

Eileen Malone

CONSTRUCTION WORKER

Deaf to the cable stretch
and snap, flash and rumble

a frizzy-haired young woman
hard hat, silver steel-tipped boots
tools on her belt clanging like batons

leaves the row of chemical toilets
behind the chain-link gate, adjusts
the belt holding up her faded jeans

isn't bothered by the urine fecal stink
unnatural hothouse sweetness

tossing an invisible cloak about her
she steps into the white turquoise air
as if into music, swaggers back

to where things get knocked down
and rebuilt by misers

old buildings sink into bang
crash, shudder of nonexistence

new buildings show off ribs
steel skeletons flank girders

she heads for the crane
something big and dumb
stuck in a tar pit trying to crawl out

up from the empty space
from which everything emanates

not from what is
but from what is yet to be created.

Carolina Morales

TO MY ELEVENTH DRAFT

Nerve grinder, inept definer,

jive-time,
nickel and dime, two
timin' rhymer,

this time, slimy little whiner,
I'd like

to kick your behind,
give you a shiner, slap

you flat into a binder,
ship your butt
to Indochina

but, somewhere inside,
a patient, diligent

writer resides, and I'm
tryin' to find her.

Pat Gallagher Sassone

WHAT'S THAT SOUND?

In factories, offices and stores,
the echo of a 240-year-old American history.
Working women craning from the bottom, sliding to the
    middle, competing near the top.
That glass ceiling is about to crash.
The pinnacle of power in arm's reach of a woman.
What's that silence?
The moment of a defeat words inadequately describe.
The mute chorus of American women wondering when, if ever.

PEOPLE HAVE THE POWER:

Nasty Women Poets on Social Justice & Political Protest

DIGITAL ANTHROPOLOGISTS FIND
OUR HASHTAGS

Dear #AltonSterling, Your face reminds me of
my brother. My son. My older cousin, Van. My first boyfriend,
the only one who ever asked me to a dance. No golden grill,
but he was kind. Still. #ThisAgain.

@POTUS facebooked today, "These fatal shootings are not isolated."
Retweet #BatonRouge Retweet #FalconHeights
    Dear #PhilandoCastile
After four gunshots, your girlfriend asked, "Where is my
daughter?"
"Where is my daughter?" while recording, "Keep your hands up!"
#ForABustedTailLight like #WalterLScott.

#ThisAgain.

Facebook: I wish Obama was a Magic Negro.
In his last six months he could wave his wand and #MakeItStop.

@BlackTwitterGuru: "Drake is awake. He is 'concerned' now
about his own family, even. #WeSeeYouBro"
    Dear #AltonSterling,
I am sorry that I haven't done enough, don't want to hear
more stories, can't remember *all*
the names.

Twitter: "Advice for allies, if you want to help, do,
and do not ask a black person how to fix
white supremacists or these murders."

Dear #TravonMartin, @BBC is tweeting Beyoncé today,
"WE ARE SICK AND TIRED . . ." They report that
a black woman protesting at the mic in Baton Rouge asked,
"How many of you really wish you were white?"
       They said, "Remarkable!"

@RandomlyComfortable: Say NO to trial by media!
       NO! to black paranoia. #BeColorBlind Wait for the facts.
       For. The. Facts.

Dear #JordanDavis, Today is like—Dear #JonathanFerrell,
       I have a qu—
Dear #MichaelBrown, What happ—Dear #TamirRice,
       You were so young and . . .
Dear #SandraBland, If only the cop . . .
       Dear #MotherEmmanuelAME, I will rememb—
       Dear #NimaliHenry and #FreddieGray, I believe that it . . .
Dear #ICantBreathe a.k.a. #EricGarner, I—We—I am sorry
       because . . . more names.

Desiré Aguirre

DANCING HORSES

The election passed like golden leaves falling.
The world didn't stop, although the peso crashed.
But horses continued to elegantly dance before winter's snow.

In early times, horses danced graceful as snow.
In reality, they were trained as weapons of war.
But modern warfare drops bombs that fly faster than
        golden leaves falling.

I tell myself that four years of the trumpet shall pass,
that I will not hide in the dungeon or shake with fear,
that I will be as strong and resilient as a horse dancing
        before winter's snow.

My daughter called in tears walking to work.
An ordinary day made quite unordinary
with wishy-washy blue skies but not one golden leaf falling.

We will be nasty women, I tell her.
We will stand together and sing in glorious harmony.
We will sit side by side on painted horses dancing
        in winter's snow.

We will don colorful clothes and mismatched socks
and braid golden fall leaves into our hair.
Our tears will unfurl, creating
a blanket of white snow for dancing horses.

Melissa Balmain

DOROTHY PARKER'S GHOST WEIGHS IN ON THE "NEW POLITICAL CLIMATE"

Men get free passes
For grabbing girls' asses.

FAILED SPELLS

For almost four years, I lived in Rod Serling's hometown,
and the sun would disappear and stay gone, as if East
Seattle or lower Alaska claimed me. All the days circled
so mundane, drab as bus stops, but that quiet sounded
nothing like the hush after election day, almost as quiet
as pipeline contracts and murderers acquitted by mistrials
or paid leaves, death older than all. Remember we can't
drink oil, and oil makes money, but no one can eat either,
even if pennies rest their tinny savor on tongues like blood.

The sidewalks of Washington Heights and Brooklyn feel
solid, too damned quiet before spray-painted swastikas,
ripped hijabs, and burned churches can be tallied. What
can be said to the man with access to the button when he
is more concerned with tweets? He'd kill birds for a profit,
collateral damage. What country is this? The land where
company towns and segregation threaded the railroads
and cotton fields, but this same earth, this cursed and
blessed soil is where we say no. The fields where promises
of powerful fools will bow some, but promises are destined
to go brittle, break into failed spells that will be uttered again.

Carolyn Breedlove

WITH YOU ALWAYS: IRAN 2009

The blood will be with you always,
the smell and burn of the teargas,
the smoke of the fires in the streets,
your chants, the shouting, the feel
of the stones in your hand,
how you ran, how the motorcycles
charged among you till you learned
to overpower even them, bring them down
and burn them. Not just in dreams
but in the days you will see
how you held hands, locked arms,
supported and carried, were supported,
were carried. And the blood. And their eyes
around you, above the masks, the scarves,
as they were beaten, as they were dragged away,
determined—as they wept.
Even when you close your eyes
you will see, forever, green
and the red. You will remember it all.
One day you will look in the mirror,
startled that you are old, amazed
at all the years gone, that you are gray,
that you could be parent—grandparent—
to those who died while young, amazed
you lived, when any day then you might not have,
amazed at what you all did, at your courage,
your steadfastness, at the blood.

Kim Bridgford

WHY EMILY DICKINSON WOULD MARCH ON WASHINGTON

Unsuffocate—release Before—
Because some things you leave home for.

With more than jam—and You are ready
Because sometimes a basket's heavy.

Because your dashes work—away—
Because you have a door—Cachet—

Because you find you write to sew
Both Life—and death. You have to go.

Twyla Hansen

BAD HAIR DAY

I'm having a bad hair day. Actually, it's more like several
    bad hair months.
Linda cuts my hair in her home. She used to be my son's family
    stylist, and
my daughter-in-law's family stylist before that. Where else could
    I mump on
about family history and politics?

I get weepy thinking of the Clinton years
when my granddaughters were little. I do not recall bad hair days
    back then.
Since I've been seeing Linda, we've jumped from good to Dubya,
    back to good,
and now on to the very worst kind of chump.

                    I've had bad haircuts before, like
when my brother chopped it—then dumped it all on me—during
    the Ike era:
cold war bump-up, nuclear warheads humping toward Omaha.
    Will we again
pump up for another stand-off?

                 Linda likes to fuss with my hair after a trim,
clump on layers of product, plump it into soft curls. Says it
    makes me look more
"professional." Me? I just don't want to look like a frump. I hate
    spending hours
in front of the mirror.

I blame it all on Trump. My last appointment was before
the election, but I didn't notice the unevenness until after.

I mean, we grumped
in disbelief at the outrageous things he'd said: "loser" POWs
　　and dead soldiers,
"murderer" and "rapist" Mexicans, "nasty" women, and mocking
　　the disabled.

The more we thumped, the faster she worked those scissors.
　　And talk about bad
hair—that orange mop—we just can't believe it's not the finest fake
　　a billionaire
can buy. Which leads me back to my woefully lopsided
　　and lump-layered locks,
slowly growing out.

　　　"The difference between a good haircut and a bad one
is about six weeks," my husband used to say before he went
　　semi-bald.
Trouble is, I'm stumped. I've fallen and can't get up from
　　this huge slump.
Mine will take more like four years.

Marianne Kunkel

LIPSTICK TO HILLARY

Your make-up crew convinces you to keep me
in your pantsuit pocket. I fade fast, and a touch-up
after a long speech and some hasty sips of water
turns your lips raspberry red again. You joke my tint
is called Reassuring Red because a poll of likely voters
prefers me to your real lip color—mottled beige.
I've felt your teeth, crowned, wide, while en route
to Coral Springs to meet the mayor; our car
swerved and your rushed hand slipped, sending me skiing
through your half-open half-pout—how every woman puckers
her mouth for me. Sometimes I'm proud we're close,
when floods of fingers flutter over guardrails
just to graze you. Sometimes I cry for a different owner,
a shy freshman to delicately glide me along her lips,
blot me, gloss me, trust me to hook the heart
of her horny lab partner. *If only it were a cigarette,*
you joke to your make-up crew then drop me
in your pocket; the debate begins and Mr. Trump
waves his arms, describing a border wall.
You carefully scrawl small words, your black pen
thin and beveled like me, yet you hold it much longer—
it's a rose and your hand's a vase, snug, graceful.
When you say your opponent hides crimes in his tax returns
he shouts *Wrong wrong* until you pause and seal your lips,
no longer raspberry red but ashen apple. You don't
wear the kiss-me face of a string bikini model
but as he keeps interjecting, you don't look rattled either.
This, finally, I understand: only I know when I'm on
my last twist, one sunny coat away from empty,
just like you don't show when your patience is thinning.

Amy Lemmon

THE DONALD'S SECRET CLONE

keeps his nose to the grindstone
and runs a tidy real estate operation
in Queens, growing it modestly to include
the other boroughs. He marries, once for love
and once, in midlife crisis, for the usual reasons.
After the second divorce he stays single,
escorting a series of graying, zaftig brunettes
to charity affairs and ribbon-cuttings.
He is a minor miracle, a businessman
with a heart, donating time and money
to rescued animals and refugees, and when
he makes a modest run for City Council (he'd
never dream of being Mayor, let alone
President) learns Spanish to converse
with his constituency and never even mentions
his *pinga.* No one pays him to be on television,
no one lampoons him in a satirical novel,
no one even invents a magazine called *Spy.*
The clone takes on the karma of the original,
pays his taxes, spends more time with his children
and less time on his hair, close-cropped
to a style both modest and age-appropriate,
respectably silver with only a hint of his native red.

Amy Miller

I AM OVER HERE SOBBING

Under an infinite dome of expanding
night, the crickets recording
a high of one hundred, Hillary Clinton
is winning California and standing
with her daughter and wearing,
near as I can tell, a flak jacket
under that awkward coat and I'm
thinking, Bill with his hand in hers,
we don't even know what
to call him, a president's husband,
we don't have the language
for it yet, and already I'm thinking
of who would troll me on Facebook
if I said that, of who would fire off
a foot-long rant—*Monsanto*
and *shrill* and *bought* and *hawk*—
and who would make a blowjob joke
out of that term we have yet to invent—
first husband? first man?—all clichés
taken already—and the all-caps
of the world are shouting
again in my head, even
my mother who said *if you want*
horses, marry a man with horses,
and I am over here sobbing
at the history writing itself
and for once I am singing
the national anthem, that part
at the baseball game where I normally
lower my eyes in silence, my hand
nowhere near my heart, as I try

not to think of bursting or rockets
or bombs but instead rest my eyes
on the grass with its millions
of green blades patiently growing.

Lesléa Newman

THE COMING STORM

Outside sheets of rain
Inside sheets of satin

Outside pounding sleet
Inside pounding hearts

Outside temperatures fall
Inside temperatures rise

Outside bare branches
Inside naked limbs

Outside shivering with cold
Inside quivering with heat

Outside slick roads
Inside slick skin

Outside heavy snow
Inside heavy breathing

Outside slippery sidewalks
Inside slippery fingers

Outside glistening fields
Inside glistening bodies

Outside howl of wind
Inside howl of joy

Outside nasty weather
Inside nasty women

Jules Nyquist

NASTY WOMAN PANTOUM

*For Hillary Rodham Clinton, Janet Reno, Mabel Dodge Luhan,
Georgia O'Keeffe, Erica Jong, Joan Baez, Victoria Woodhull,
and Gloria Steinem. The fight for women continues.*

I suppose I could have stayed home, baked cookies, hosted teas
but I've been labeled a nasty woman.
If I was elected, I could have slept with an ex-President,
the First Dude would have played sax full time.

I am a nasty woman.
Janet Reno's mother wrestled alligators.
The First Dude would have played sax full time.
Georgia said if I painted that mountain long enough I would own it.

Janet Reno's mother wrestled alligators.
My life broke in two right there, Mabel.
Georgia said if I painted that mountain long enough I would own it.
I am proud to wear pantsuits.

My life broke in two, Mabel.
I am fearless of the far side of fifty, Erica.
I am proud to wear pantsuits with zippers,
flying first class without fear, I'll escape to an island, I've had enough.

I am fearless, long past the far side of fifty.
Joan didn't sleep with any man who had a draft card.
flying first class without fear I will continue to work with children.
I could have been your Madam President; Victoria Woodhull
     was counting on me.

Joan didn't sleep with any man who had a draft card.
A woman without a man is like a fish without a bicycle.
I could have been your Madam President; Victoria Woodhull
     was counting on me.
I would have kept abortion legal; honey, if men could
     get pregnant it would be a sacrament.

A woman without a man is like a fish without a bicycle.
I wasn't elected, but I can still sleep with the ex-President.
I would have kept abortion legal; honey, if men could
     get pregnant it would be a sacrament.
I suppose I could have stayed home, baked cookies, hosted teas.

Lyndi Bell O'Laughlin

INAUGURAL ADDRESS

"No one will buy the cow
if you give the milk
away for free," Mama said.
So discover the price
for a gallon of milk,
note how it can become
the rough equivalent
of a feminine soul,
substitute currency
in real world economics,
having to do with laundry,
meals, the casting
of a particular shadow,
cooperation,
and the shoebox of choices,
hidden on the closet floor
beneath a tie rack
of ideas and dreams.
Handy, should she want
to pull one down
and strangle herself.

May be additional cost
soon, a few days out
from the hour
the grabber of pussies
sings his oath of office
before setting about the work,
since "There has to be a punishment."

Not every pussy will line up.
Some won't purr,
have escaped into the jungle,
hone sharp edges,
say
fuck the cow
fuck the milk
fuck the farmer.

Dzvinia Orlowsky

PUSSY RIOT/WANT/DON'T/WANT

I thought you were a catch phrase for the *not tonight, oh yes*
tonight, but not two nights in a row!
of late middle age

how else to say it:

the thatched roofs are on fire
& the villagers have fled

except this woman
whom you left behind,

her skirt rising in flames,
wild heat,

a wreckage of *K-Y* and Oil of Olay

• • •

O graying fraying housebound hive,
you're not my problem,

though I will admit

your spreading reflection in the hand-held mirror
looks, this year,

don't make me say it,

wiser—

if not for love or song,

• • •

Can a finger dip into honey
in late January?

Can red wine stream like blood down my legs?

This afternoon, huddled against the cutting winter wind
in front of Boston's State House,
we protested

> *Putin must go!*
> *Yanokovich is a cesspool!*

while you, Prison punk prayer,
turn the world's attention
to

holy
hooliganism!

I thought you were a catch phrase for the want-don't want
of late middle age,

(oh pussy, what a riot, I had you all wrong)

THE PRESIDENT-ELECT SPEAKS

"You can always go to another
state" to have your abortion
just so long as you're rich,
have a nanny to watch your

kids, can take off from your
job, have a ride available
or your own car, aren't
living at home or needing

to hide the procedure. Yes
affluent women could fly
to Puerto Rico while the rest
of us were doing it to ourselves,

dying of back alley butchery,
bleeding to death, left sterile
from botched operations,
yes, we can always just die,

Mr. Trump, and many mothers
will be leaving their children
to be raised by others, many
teenagers will drop out of school,

many women will die alone
in their bloody beds. It will
be just the way you like it
for women who dare to choose.

JOB (WAR SURVIVOR'S GUILT)

and in the denial of the words. I know how as latex-wrapped fingers press close to see inside grandmother will press lips tight together. grandmother will press sickness sounds down deep deep down. to push back the rising of aunt's voice throat cut bled out by latex-gloved hands *back home in Amin's war* until the sounding rings out in tiny brown bead shapes rung round brown skin. and grandmother will press fingers soft to one, all. a silent hail mary, a silent grace.

Stacey Waite

DEADLOCKED

The Nebraska Board of Education
member Maris Bentley says
we need to protect our kids
from the harmful queer agenda.
The board itself, deadlocked,
three on three.

Maris Bentley fears
that "choose your own
bathroom" makes gender
"too loosey goosey"
like each urination
will become a choose your own
adventure—she's afraid
kids will change
their genders daily,
afraid the sexual predators
will come out of the woodwork
like dirty disobedient termites,
gnawing at the thin panel
of values she's taught
her four kids
her nine grandchildren
the hundreds of students
to whom she has been
a counselor. Maris Bentley,
there's so much I want to say
but I know it will do no good.

You're deadlocked, after all,
like happened to me once
driving through Pennsylvania,
when a man's hands
were deadlocked into my throat
as I left a public restroom.
I can't read the way you want me to,
Maris Bentley. My gender is deadlocked, too,
deadlocked in the space between man and woman,
chromosomes deadlocked, hormones deadlocked,
body deadlocked, haircut deadlocked,
others like me, locked dead in their bodies,
locked dead in your language,
locked
dead.

WOMAN DANCING ON HER SON'S COFFIN, NEW ORLEANS, 1995

from a black and white photograph
at the House of Dance and Feathers

She is not
        in black not
        weeping, not leaning
against someone as she staggers,
                drunk with grief, no—

She dances on top
        of her son's coffin
        outside the Lafitte Projects
where he was gunned down.
She dances and dances
                unbending, limbs thrashing
        like Kali
                on Shiva's ashen body.

Gray clothes—
        are they sweats?—
sway in the sun-blasted noon,
        her two living boys
        make music around her:
D-Boy gone
        who that killed D-Boy who
first told her the news? She can't,
        some funneled shape
                his horn won't blow.

No lace,
    no shawl across her shoulders.
Bare-armed, back cocked,
      ass out, she dances, yes—

—another thud of percussion—

I, no   she
    grunts,
       pushing him out
ripping open at Charity,
       fluorescent lights
       backlighting his arched shape

—bright slash of the trumpet—

he burns with fever,
     laughs at ice
  tracing
  the pouting lips

    late July, night blooming jasmine
     thick in the mouth

    I grab another sliver
     —slap of snare—

—no, she does,
    it's her boy,

a number now
  pushing up the murder graph
  like a thermometer

      oh mama mama

Men hauling the casket bend
at the knees
        not from weight
                but from bass thump,
from tuba's
    fat momentum.

        Her sweats shift
soft and loose
    as they play it loose and mean,
        a threat in the throb
the trombone moans
                she's gone

past shiver
    past flash of brass glint
        & casket shine underneath her feet

        she shakes her head—look:
           she's turning to look
                into everyone's face.

Janet E. Aalfs, poet laureate emeritus of Northampton, MA, and founder/director of Peace Arts at Valley Women's Martial Arts, is a radical (root) instigator of peace, justice, and freedom for all. Her most recent collection of poems is *Bird of a Thousand Eyes* (Levellers Press).

Nordette N. Adams of New Orleans, LA, has an MFA in Creative Writing from the University of New Orleans as well as an MA in English. She accepts some praise and blame for the OED removing "a rabid feminist" as its top usage example for the adjective "rabid."

Kim Addonizio is the author of seven poetry collections, two novels, two short story collections, and two books on writing poetry. Her collection *Tell Me* was a National Book Award Finalist. Her latest books are *Mortal Trash: Poems* (Norton) and a memoir-in-essays, *Bukowski in a Sundress* (Penguin).

Kelli Russell Agodon is the author of six books and the cofounder of Two Sylvias Press. Her most recent book, *Hourglass Museum,* was a finalist for the Washington State Book Awards. She never apologizes for having dessert or a second glass of wine.

Kathleen Aguero has been a nasty woman poet since her first book publication in 1977. Her latest collection is *After That* (Tiger Bark). She teaches in the low-residency MFA program at Pine Manor College and in Changing Life Through Literature (an alternative sentencing program), and conducts Creative Writing for Caregiver workshops.

Desiré Aguirre lives in Idaho. She belongs to a women's writing group that inspires her, has a blog for bereaved parents, and writes for *Idaho Magazine.* A singer/songwriter, she plays in the string band *Ruff Shodd.* When she's not writing or playing music, she rides her horses into the mountains.

Liz Ahl has a slight preference for "surly" over "nasty," but will happily respond to either. She hones her poker skills and conducts the rest of her nasty agenda in the semi-wilds of New Hampshire. Her collection of poems *Beating the Bounds* is due out in 2017 from Hobblebush Books.

Ann Alexander's dark past included many years as an advertising copywriter in London before she ran away to Cornwall. She lives in Stratford-upon-Avon now, close to Shakespeare's birthplace, and grumbles about the tourists. She has four collections of poetry to her name, published by Peterloo Poets and Ward Wood.

Patsy Asuncion's *Cut on the Bias* (Laughing Fire Press, 2016) depicts her world *slant* as a bi-racial child raised by an immigrant father and WWII vet. Publications include *The New York Times* (online), *vox poetica, The New Verse News, Cutthroat Journal, Snapdragon,* and *Reckless Writing.* Patsy promotes diversity through her open mic and community initiatives.

Cynthia Atkins is the author of *Psyche's Weathers* and *In The Event of Full Disclosure. Still Life With God* is forthcoming in 2018. Her poems have appeared in *Alaska Quarterly Review, BOMB, Cleaver Magazine, Del Sol Review, Hermeneutic Chaos, North American Review,* and *Verse Daily.* She teaches Creative Writing at Blue Ridge Community College.

Anne Babson practices her nastiness in New Orleans. Her prizewinning book *White Trash Pantheon* is available in independent bookstores and online. She wrote the libretto to a nasty opera about nasty women called *Lotus Lives,* which has been performed in cities across the country.

Stacey Balkun is the author of three poetry chapbooks. A finalist for the 2016 Center for Women Writer's Rita Dove Award, she has work in *Crab Orchard Review, Muzzle, Bayou,* and others. Stacey serves as chapbook series editor for Sundress Publications and teaches poetry online at Poetry Barn.

Melissa Balmain is editor of *Light,* a journal of comic verse (www. lightpoetrymagazine.com). Her poetry collection *Walking In on People* (winner of the Able Muse Book Award) gets nasty on subjects ranging from bras to boyfriends to parenthood and prunes.

Devon Balwit is a teacher/poet living in Portland, OR. She has two chapbooks, *How the Blessed Travel* (Maverick Duck Press) and *Forms Most Marvelous* (forthcoming from dancing girl press). Her poems have appeared in *The Cincinnati Review, The Stillwater Review, Red Earth Review, The Tule Review, Sow's Ear Poetry Review, Rattle,* and elsewhere.

Wendy Barker's sixth collection, *One Blackbird at a Time* (BkMk Press, 2015) won the Ciardi Poetry Prize. Her poetry has appeared in hundreds of journals and anthologies, including *Best American Poetry.* Recipient of an NEA and Rockefeller fellowships, she's taught for fifty-one fuckin' years, including the last thirty-five, at UT San Antonio.

Carol Barrett has supported women graduate students for over forty years. She earned two Ph.D.s—the first in Clinical Psychology, where she worked with widowed women, and the second in Creative Writing, where she revisioned the Hebrew Bible text of Esther. See her book of poems, *Calling the Bones.*

Judith Barrington has published four poetry collections, most recently *The Conversation* (Salmon Poetry). In the 70s, she lived in London and was part of the movement as a staff person for the Women's Liberation Workshop. As a nasty woman, she defaced posters and indulged in property damage as well as demonstrations and marches.

Tina Barry's writing appears in numerous literary magazines and anthologies including *Drunken Boat, The American Poetry Journal,* and *The Best Small Fictions 2016.* She is an editor and writing tutor. Tina lives with her husband and two nasty cats in upstate New York.

Jan Beatty's books include *Jackknife: New and Selected Poems, The Switching/Yard, Red Sugar, Boneshaker,* and *Mad River,* all published by the University of Pittsburgh Press. Beatty worked as a waitress for fifteen years, and as a welfare caseworker, an abortion counselor, and a social worker and teacher in a maximum-security prison.

Patricia Behrens is a lawyer living in Manhattan who believes in free speech and the power of women's voices. Her poetry has appeared in *American Arts Quarterly, The Main Street Rag, Mom Egg Review, Poetry Porch, The Same,* and elsewhere.

DeMisty D. Bellinger teaches Creative Writing, Women's Studies, and African-American Studies at Fitchburg State University. Her writing has appeared many places, including *The Rumpus, Necessary Fiction,* and *Forklift, Ohio.* Her chapbook *Rubbing Elbows* is available from Finishing Line Press. She lives in Massachusetts with her husband and twin daughters.

Margo Berdeshevsky, NYC-born, writes in high-boot, darkling Paris. Her precipice-new collection from Glass Lyre Press is *Before the Drought.* There's also *Between Soul & Stone, But a Passage in the Wilderness,* and *Beautiful Soon Enough.* She is now striding in London, Paris, New York City, or somewhere light in the world.

Tara Betts is the author of *Break the Habit* (Trio House Press, 2016) and *Arc & Hue* (Willow Books, 2009). Tara is co-editor of *The Beiging of America: Personal Narratives About Being Mixed Race in the 21ˢᵗ Century* (2Leaf Press). She teaches at the University of Illinois-Chicago.

Katie Bickham was raised in the Red South as a Republican Evangelical. Nevertheless, she persisted and became nasty. Her book *The Belle Mar* was published by LSU Press and her work has appeared widely in journals and anthologies.

Diann Blakely's idea for a "Bad Belles" panel of women poets at a past Southern Festival of Books (which included your nasty editors) was one of many predecessors for this anthology. She died young in 2014, but left us *Lost Addresses: New & Selected Poems* (Salmon, 2017). Her fierce spirit is greatly missed.

Julie E. Bloemeke is an introverted subversive whose poetry manuscript, *Slide to Unlock,* explores our perceived boundaries of intimacy through technology. She is currently working on a second manuscript while waiting for the first to cross the publishing transom. Her poems have appeared in numerous journals and anthologies.

Andrea Blythe bides her time waiting for the apocalypse by writing speculative poetry and fiction. Her work has appeared or is forthcoming in *Rogue Agent, Literary Orphans, Yellow Chair Review, Nonbinary Review, Linden Avenue,* and *Strange Horizons.* She serves as associate editor for Zoetic Press and is a member of the Science Fiction Poetry Association.

Emily Bobo is the author of *Fugue* (Lost Horse Press, 2009) and editor of *Bobo Books* (Hemlock Press, 2016), a nonprofit project turning poems into sandwiches for public school kids. She teaches writing to single moms, ex-cons, and military vets at Ivy Tech Community College.

Emma Bolden is the author of *med(i)tations* (Noctuary Press, 2016) and *Maleficae* (GenPop Books, 2013). Her work has appeared in *The Best American Poetry* and *The Best Small Fictions.* She received a 2017 Creative Writing Fellowship from the NEA and lives in Alabama with a nasty pussycat named Gertrude Stein.

Andi Boyd grew up in South Louisiana and resides in San Antonio, TX. She holds a B.A. in English from Northwestern State University and an MFA in Poetry from Texas State University. Her writing has previously appeared in *Gulf Coast, Narrative Magazine, Black Warrior Review, Drunken Boat,* and others.

Carolyn Breedlove edited and annotated *A Glorious Day: The Journal of a Central Louisiana Governess,1853-1854.* Her poems have appeared in *Comstock Review, Wisconsin Review, New Millennium Writings,* and *Maple Leaf Rag,* among others. Finishing Line Press published her chapbook, *Just Following the River.* She is currently finishing a novel.

Shirley J. Brewer serves as poet-in residence at Carver Center for the Arts & Technology in Baltimore. Recent poems appear in *Barrow Street, Poetry East, Slant,* and *Gargoyle.* Books include: *A Little Breast Music, After*

Words, and *Bistro in Another Realm.* Shirley released her inner nasty after Election Day, 2016.

Kim Bridgford is the director of Poetry by the Sea: A Global Conference; the editor of *Mezzo Cammin,* an online formalist journal by women; and the founder of the Mezzo Cammin Women Poets Timeline Project, a database of women poets. She is known as "America's First Lady of Form."

Jennifer Bullis started out nice. But in the 80s she attended a former men's college where some faculty still opposed admission of women. In the 90s, she survived further academic hazing and earned a doctorate thanks to second-wave feminists. In the 2000s, she wrote *Impossible Lessons.* She remains pissed.

Cathleen Calbert's poetry and prose have appeared in publications including *Ms. Magazine, The New Republic, The New York Times,* and *The Paris Review.* She is the author of four books of poetry: *Lessons in Space, Bad Judgment, Sleeping with a Famous Poet,* and *The Afflicted Girls.* Her many awards include *The Nation* Discovery Award and a Pushcart Prize.

Hélène Cardona's books include, most recently, *Life in Suspension* and *Dreaming My Animal Selves,* and the translations *Beyond Elsewhere* (Gabriel Arnou-Laujeac), winner of a Hemingway Grant; *Ce que nous portons* (Dorianne Laux); *The Birnam Wood* by her father, Jóse Manuel Cardona; and Walt Whitman's *Civil War Writings* for *Whitman Web.*

Lauren Carpenter received her MFA from Purdue University. She has previously been published in *The Lumberyard* and *The Greensboro Review.* She currently resides in Columbus, OH, where she works for a healthcare technology company.

Sarah Carson's work has appeared in *Christian Century, DIAGRAM, Guernica, The Minnesota Review,* and *The New Orleans Review,* among others, She is the author of two poetry collections, *Poems in Which You Die* (BatCat Press) and *Buick City* (Mayapple Press) and several chapbooks. Born and raised in Michigan, she lives in Chicago with her two dogs.

Susana H. Case is the author of five books of poetry, most recently *Drugstore Blue* from Five Oaks Press and *4 Rms w Vu* from Mayapple Press, as well as four chapbooks. She is a professor and program coordinator for New York Institute of Technology in New York City.

Anne Champion is the author of *Reluctant Mistress, The Good Girl is Always a Ghost,* and *The Dark Length Home.* Her poems have appeared in *Verse Daily, Prairie Schooner, Salamander, Epiphany Magazine,* and elsewhere.

She has won an Academy of American Poets Prize and a Barbara Deming Memorial Grant. She teaches at Wheelock College in Boston.

As a nasty woman, **Kelly Cherry** has published twenty-five books, ten chapbooks, and two books of translations. Book # 26, *Temporium,* comes out in the fall of 2017. She remembers when few men would read poetry by women, and is happy to have been among those who have helped change their minds.

Patricia Clark learned about nasty women from her mother, Norma (Collins) Clark, and believes in political protest through words, action, and the ballot. Her most recent book is *The Canopy.* New work appears in *Asheville Poetry Review* and *Plume 5* and is forthcoming in *Prairie Schooner* and *Adirondack Review.* She organized readings on 1/21/17 to protest the inauguration.

Cathryn Cofell is a fierce arts advocate, launching the Wisconsin Poet Laureate Commission and its endowment fund, the WFOP Chapbook Prize, and a long-running reading series in Appleton, WI. She has a collection, *Sister Satellite,* six chapbooks, and a CD to her name, but no restraining order. Yet.

Emily Rose Cole is the author of a chapbook, *Love and a Loaded Gun,* forthcoming from Minerva Rising Press. Her favorite topics to write about include doomed birds, rewritten fairytales, and dangerous women, especially witches. She holds an MFA from Southern Illinois University Carbondale and a Ph.D. from the University of Cincinnati.

Maryann Corbett *(translation of Christine de Pizan)* earned a doctorate in medieval literature and expected to be teaching Beowulf and Chaucer. Instead, she spent thirty-five years working for the Minnesota Legislature. Her poems have been published in many journals, ranging from the very upright *Christianity* to the not-so-upright *Shit Creek Review.*

Barbara Crooker has been marching for peace and social justice since 1962 (a "Ban the Bomb" rally) and can't believe she's still protesting this shit. She was proud to have worked on the Clinton campaign, and is the author of eight books of poetry, including *Les Fauves* (C&R Press, 2017).

Kym Cunningham has been published in dozens of journals, none of which seem to mind her penchant for expletives. When she is not scrawling offensive metaphors, she enjoys rolling in the dirt with her dog, Truffle Monster, training in mixed martial arts activities, and participating in other unladylike activities. She does not like being told to smile.

Julie Cyr has been published in *Smoky Quartz, Five 2 One Magazine,* and *Blood and Thunder Journal,* and has work forthcoming in *Broad River Review.* She was a finalist for the 2016 Rash Award in Poetry. She holds an MFA in Poetry from Lesley University, and currently works as an editorial assistant for Surreal Poetics. She lives in southern New Hampshire with her husband and two sons.

Heidi Czerwiec earned her nasty woman cred by persisting against online misogyny with her essay "Anatomy of an Outrage" at *Roar* and her poetry chapbook *Self-Portrait as Bettie Page.* Other chapbooks are: *A Bakken Boom Cycle* and *A is for A-ke, The Chinese Monster.* She also edited *North Dakota is Everywhere: An Anthology of Contemporary North Dakota Poets.*

Angela Decker is a freelance writer and morning news announcer for southern Oregon's local NPR Station. Her poems have appeared in *African American Voices, Comstock Review, Hip Mama, The Wisconsin Review,* and others. Her chapbook, *Splendid Catastrophe,* was published by Finishing Line Press. She lives with her husband, two big-hearted sons, and too many pets.

Kendra DeColo is the author of *My Dinner with Ron Jeremy* (Third Man Books, 2016) and *Thieves in the Afterlife,* which was selected by Yusef Komunyakaa for the 2013 Saturnalia Books Poetry Prize. Her poems and essays appear in *Gulf Coast, Ninth Letter, Verse Daily, VIDA, Bitch Media,* and elsewhere.

Lisa DeSiro lives in Cambridge, MA, and works for a nonprofit organization. Her other nasty accomplishments include a chapbook, *Grief Dreams* (White Knuckle Press, 2017), poems published in many journals and set to music by several composers, degrees in creative writing and piano, and a black belt in Taekwondo.

Emari DiGiorgio is She-tex. Her debut collection, *The Things a Body Might Become,* is forthcoming from Five Oaks Press in 2017. She is the recipient of the 2016 Auburn Witness Poetry Prize honoring Jake Adam York.

Sharon Dolin is the author of six poetry collections—most recently, *Manual for Living* and *Whirlwind,* both from the University of Pittsburgh Press. She directs and teaches in Writing About Art in Barcelona each June. Her motto is "nasty is as nasty does."

Lisa Dordal, author of *Mosaic of the Dark,* teaches at Vanderbilt University. She is a Pushcart Prize nominee and the recipient of an Academy of American Poets Prize. Her poetry has appeared in *Best New*

Poets, CALYX, The Greensboro Review, Vinyl Poetry, and *The Journal of Feminist Studies in Religion.*

Amy Dryansky's second book, *Grass Whistle* (Salmon), received the Massachusetts Book Award for poetry. Her first, *How I Got Lost So Close to Home,* was published by Alice James. Her poems appear in a variety of journals and anthologies. She works at Hampshire College, and is poet laureate of Northampton, Massachusetts.

Carla Drysdale is a Canadian poet who lives in France. Her books are *Inheritance* and *Little Venus.* Her poems have appeared in *PRISM, LIT, The Fiddlehead, Literary Mama, Cleaver Magazine,* Paris Press's *Spiraling,* and elsewhere. A nominee for Bettering American Poetry in 2015, she won *PRISM's* Earle Birney prize in 2014.

Rachel Eisler grew up in New York City and studied writing at Yale and Johns Hopkins. She currently teaches at an all-girls' school and a women's prison in Maryland. She was a finalist for a Pushcart Prize in 2016, and her poems appear in *upstreet* and *Little Patuxent Review.*

Julie R. Enszer is the author of *Avowed, Lilith's Demons, Sisterhood,* and *Hand Made Love.* She is editor of *The Complete Works of Pat Parker* and *Milk & Honey: A Celebration of Jewish Lesbian Poetry.*

Emily Dickinson said, "If your Nerve deny you—/ Go above your Nerve." **Susan J. Erickson** says that is her definition of being nasty. Therefore, the women in her book, *Lauren Bacall Shares a Limousine,* qualify as nasty women.

Anna M. Evans is a crusader for transparency and justice who speaks to power, most recently by running as a Democrat for Township Committee in a red New Jersey town. She was so "nasty" her Republican opponents tried to lock her up.

Kelly Everding lives in Minneapolis and works for the nonprofit organization Rain Taxi, which publishes *Rain Taxi Review of Books.* Off hours are spent knitting pink pussy hats and demonstrating for women's reproductive health rights. Her chapbook, *Strappado for the Devil,* was published by Etherdome Press in 2004.

Alexis Rhone Fancher's books, *Enter Here* and *How I Lost My Virginity to Michael Cohen,* break new erotic ground and explore the true meaning of power. Find her poems everywhere from stashed under your mattress to *The Best American Poetry 2016.* Her photos are published worldwide.

Poet, performer, and educator **Corie Feiner** was the 2011 poet laureate of Bucks County. She has been published in numerous anthologies and journals and is the author of the poetry collection *Radishes into Roses* and the children's book *Who Was Born at Home?*

Marta Ferguson has been the bitch behind Wordhound Writing & Editing Services LLC for fifteen years. She's the smart-ass co-editor of *Drawn to Marvel: Poems from the Comic Books* (Minor Arcana Press) and the notoriously smirky author of much nasty poetry, including a chapbook from Main Street Rag.

Gina Ferrara's collections include *The Size of Sparrows* (Finishing Line Press, 2006), *Ethereal Avalanche* (Trembling Pillow Press, 2009), *Amber Porch Light* (CW Books, 2013) and *Carville: Amid Moss and Resurrection Fern* (FLP, 2014). Her latest, *Fitting the Sixth Finger: Poems Inspired by the Paintings of Marc Chagall*, was published by Kelsey Books.

Annie Finch's most recent book of poetry is *Spells* (Wesleyan). She has just completed a new prose book, *The Witch in You: Five Directions to Your Inner Goddess,* and she is editing an anthology on abortion. She teaches in the low-res MFA program at St. Francis College in Brooklyn.

Mary Florio's award-winning work has appeared in the *Paterson Literary Review*. She has collaborated with book artist Miriam Schaer on two poems, "The Posture Queen" and "Cinderella Ever After," which were selected as part of a book arts exhibition sponsored by the CBA in NYC.

Alice Friman's latest collection is *The View from Saturn* (LSU). Her previous collection, *Vinculum,* won the 2012 Georgia Author of the Year Award in Poetry. She won a 2012 Pushcart Prize and is included in *Best American Poetry 2009.* She lives in Milledgeville, Georgia, where she is the poet-in-residence at Georgia College.

CMarie Fuhrman likes it dirty. She spends her summers wild in Idaho, her winters consulting snakes she encountered on her adventures. She runs her dogs without leashes and keeps her toenails unpainted. Part Phryne Fisher and part Calamity Jane, she holds her poems at gunpoint, then offers them a Scotch.

Nola Garrett, professor emerita of Edinboro University of PA, now lives happily alone in downtown Pittsburgh. She is the author of *The Dynamite Worker's Mistress, The Pastor's Wife Considers Pinball,* and *Ledge.* She has received a residency at Yaddo and is posted in *The Georgia Review Vault.*

Maria Mazziotti Gillan writes: "Always being conscious of my foreignness, poetry gave me a way to speak for myself and other immigrants. My parents lacked money and opportunity, yet raised a doctor, a nurse, a professor, and a poet. Their grandchildren are professors, attorneys, and accountants. That is wonderful about America. The importance of immigrants is woven into its fabric."

Emma Goldman-Sherman is a playwright/poet who has walked through Customs in merely a trench coat and heels, declaring everything. Having survived her parents, incest, and childbirth, she identifies as a bisexual, non-Zionist Jew. She teaches writing and runs the 29th Street Playwrights Collective and the Write Now Workshop. Her most recent play is *Whorticulture.*

Estella Gonzalez was born and raised in East Los Angeles, which inspired her writing. Her literary influences include a long line of sin vergüenzas, including Sandra Cisneros, Michelle Serros, and Madonna. Her work has been selected for a Pushcart Prize "Special Mention" and a "Reading Notable" for *The Best American Non-Required Reading.*

Grace Gorski is a poet and preschool teacher living in St. Louis, MO. She has previously published work in *The Cargoes, The Album, Impossible Archetype,* and *The Cyborg Griffin.* When not writing, Grace enjoys making snarky comments about the patriarchy. She is a graduate of Hollins University.

Ona Gritz's collection *Geode* was a finalist for the 2013 Main Street Rag Poetry Book Award. Currently, she and her husband, Daniel Simpson, are editing an anthology/writing guide for Diode Editions. Ona plans to survive the Trump years by continuing to read, write, march, and perform radical acts of kindness.

Andrea L. Hackbarth lives in Palmer, AK, where she works as a writing tutor and piano teacher. She holds an MFA from the University of Alaska Anchorage. Some of her work can be found in *Mezzo Cammin, Temenos, Measure,* and other print and online journals.

Brittany Hailer has taught writing workshops in a women's rehabilitation center and the Allegheny County Jail. She is a freelance journalist for *Public Source* and MFA program assistant at Chatham College. Her work has appeared in *Word Riot, Barrelhouse, Hobart,* and other journals.

Gail Hanlon's poetry has appeared in *Kenyon Review, Ploughshares, Cincinnati Review, Cutbank Online, Iowa Review, Best American Poetry,* and elsewhere. She was a finalist for the Iowa Review Award (2013), a semi-finalist for the Tomaz Salamun Prize at *Verse* Magazine (2015), and a Top 25 in *Glimmer Train's* Short Story Award (2017).

Twyla Hansen believes in free speech. She also believes that speech and actions to undermine the rights of women and other marginalized people must be consistently called out for what they are: power/domination play, bullying, suppressing freedoms, etc. Together, enlightened people can do this! RESIST! Wake. Up. Get. Involved. Vote.

Marie Harris is an early member of the groundbreaking poetry cooperative Alice James Books, and has long taken pride in standing with nasty women everywhere. She was the NH poet laureate from 1999-2004. She is the author of *Your Son, Manny: A Prose Poem Memoir* (White Pine Press).

Nancy C. Harris received a B.A. and M.A. in English from Newcomb/ Tulane in New Orleans. She has organized the Maple Leaf Bar Literary Readings since the death of Everette Maddox in 1989. Her books include: *The Ape Woman Story* (Pirogue Publishing, 1989), *Mirror Wars* (Portals Press, 1999), and *Beauty Eating Beauty* (Portals Press, 2013).

Ashley Mace Havird's subversive side took root during her childhood on a tobacco farm in South Carolina. A prizewinning poet (*The Garden of the Fugitives,* Texas Review Press, 2014) and novelist (*Lightningstruck,* Mercer University Press, 2016), she scuba dives whenever possible and has yet to be arrested for poaching.

Karen Head is the author of *Sassing* (WordTech Press, 2009), *My Paris Year,* and *Shadow Boxes* (both from All Nations Press). She also creates digital poetry. She is an associate professor at Georgia Tech and the editor of *Atlanta Review.*

Amy Lee Heinlen's poetry appears in *Wicked Alice, Rogue Agent, Pretty Owl Poetry,* and elsewhere. Her poem "Light Blue" was awarded a 2016 Academy of American Poets Prize. An associate editor of *Pittsburgh Poetry Review* and member of the extremely nasty Madwomen in the Attic, she is based in Pittsburgh, Pennsylvania.

Kathleen Hellen has over two hundred publications credits, including her collection *Umberto's Night,* winner of the Jean Feldman Poetry Prize, and two chapbooks, *The Girl Who Loved Mothra* and *Pentimento.* Awards include poetry prizes from *H.O.W. Journal* and *Washington Square Review.* A former journalist and editor, she teaches in Baltimore.

Sara Henning is the author of two books of poetry, most recently *View from True North,* which won the 2017 Crab Orchard Review Open Poetry Prize and will be published by Southern Illinois University Press in 2018. Her other collections include *A Sweeter Water, Garden Effigies,* and *To Speak of Dahlias.*

Rage Hezekiah is a Cave Canem and MacDowell Fellow who earned her MFA from Emerson College. Her poems have appeared or are forthcoming in *Fifth Wednesday, Columbia Poetry Review, The Cape Rock,* and *Tampa Review,* as well as other journals and anthologies.

Michele Lent Hirsch is the author of *Invisible: How Young Women with Serious Health Issues Navigate Work, Relationships, and the Pressure to Seem Just Fine* (forthcoming from Beacon Press, 2018). Her poetry and nonfiction have appeared in *The Atlantic, The Guardian, Rattle,* and *Bellevue Literary Review.*

Katherine Hoerth is a nasty feminist who lives, writes, and teaches in deep south Texas. Her poems have been published in journals such as *Mezzo Cammin, Thank You For Swallowing,* and *Alyss Lit.* She is the author of *Goddess Wears Cowboy Boots* (Lamar University Literary Press, 2014).

Andrea Holland is a lecturer in creative writing at the University of East Anglia, Norwich, UK. Her collection of poems *Broadcasting* (Gatehouse Press, 2013) won the Norwich Commission for Poetry. Her collection *Borrowed* was published by Smith/Doorstop in 2007. She has poems in *Phoebe, Rialto, MsLexia,* and *Greensboro Review,* and often collaborates with visual artists.

Elizabeth Hope, recipient of a poetry grant and a couple of prizes, writes and lives in San Francisco's Bayview-Hunters Point.

Trish Hopkinson has always loved words—in fact, her mother tells everyone she was born with a pen in her hand. She has been published in several anthologies and journals, and her third chapbook is forthcoming from Lithic Press.

Kate Hovey first tweaked the stories she's been reading since fourth grade in three award-winning books of poetry for young readers: *Arachne Speaks, Ancient Voices,* and *Voices of the Trojan War* (Simon & Schuster). A contributor to *Women Versed in Myth: Essays on Modern Poets* (MacFarland), she continues her nasty, myth-busting ways.

Rochelle Hurt is the author of two fairly nasty poetry collections: *In Which I Play the Runaway,* winner of the Barrow Street Book Prize, 2016, and *The Rusted City* (White Pine, 2014). She holds a Ph.D. from the University of Cincinnati.

Karla Huston, Wisconsin poet laureate (2017-2018) is the author of *A Theory of Lipstick* (Main Street Rag, 2013) as well as eight chapbooks, including *Grief Bone* (Five-Oak Press, 2017). Her poems, reviews, and interviews have been published widely, including in the 2012 *Pushcart Best of the Small Presses* anthology.

Elizabeth Johnston has been fascinated with Nasty Women since her parents bought her a picture Bible when she was just seven and she opened to the story of Jezebel. Now she uses her writing to reimagine and grant voice to marginalized and vilified women like Delilah and Medusa.

Allison Joseph lives in Carbondale, IL, where she teaches at Southern Illinois University. Her books include *Mercurial* (Mayapple Press), *Mortal Rewards* (White Violet Press), *Multitudes* (Word Poetry), *The Purpose of Hands* (Glass Lyre Press), *Double Identity* (Singing Bone Press), and *What Once You Loved* (Barefoot Muse Press).

When **Marilyn Kallet** turned fifty, she composed a book of sensual love poems, *How to Get Heat Without Fire.* She told herself that if she wasn't struck by lightning, she would be able to write anything she wanted, without censorship. She's never turned back and is now the author of seventeen books, including *The Love That Moves Us* (Black Widow Press).

Donna Kaz is a multi-genre writer and author of *UNMASKED: Memoirs of a Guerilla Girl on Tour.* Along with her alter ego, Guerilla Girl Aphra Behn, she creates nasty works of art and performance to attack sexism and prove that feminists are funny at the same time.

Latina writer **Rosalie Morales Kearns** is the founder of Shade Mountain Press; the author of the novel *Kingdom of Women* (Jaded Ibis, forthcoming 2017) and the magic-realist story collection *Virgins and Tricksters* (Aqueous, 2012); and the editor of the short story anthology, *The Female Complaint: Tales of Unruly Women.*

Rose Kelleher is the author of two volumes of poetry: *Bundle o' Tinder* (Waywiser Press, 2008) and *Native Species* (2013).

Diane Kendig's five poetry collections include *Prison Terms* (forthcoming 2017). She co-edited the recent anthology *In the Company* *of Russell Atkins.* A recipient of two Ohio Arts Council Fellowships in Poetry and a Fulbright translation award, she has published poetry and prose in journals such as *J Journal, Ekphrasis,* and *Common Ground.*

Proudly nasty, **Sarah Key** has been a subversive since smashing her piggy bank for civil rights in third grade. She believes the survival of the planet depends on the education of women (*Huffington Post* essay) and loves to versify with her students in the South Bronx.

Cindy King is a nasty gal whose work appears in *Callaloo, North American Review, African American Review, American Literary Review, River Styx, TriQuarterly, Black Warrior Review,* and elsewhere. In Utah, she spreads nastiness as an assistant professor at Dixie State University and editor of *Route 7 Review.*

Robin Kirk is the author of several books on Latin America. Her short stories have been published in a number of magazines. *Peculiar Motion,* her collection of poems, is available from Finishing Line Press. She teaches human rights at Duke University.

Juanita Kirton earned her MFA from Goddard College. She is a member of Women Who Write, Inc. and the Women Reading Aloud Workshops. She directs the *Quill*Essence Writing Collective and is on the editorial staff of *Clock House Literary Magazine.* She's been published in several anthologies, is a U.S Army veteran, and rides a motorcycle.

Marianne Kunkel is the author of *The Laughing Game* (Finishing Line Press) and many published poems. She earned her Ph.D. from the University of Nebraska-Lincoln, where she served as managing editor of *Prairie Schooner.* She is currently an assistant professor at Missouri Western University and editor-in-chief of *The Mochila Review.*

Melissa Kwasny is the author of six books of poetry, most recently *Where Outside the Body is the Soul Today* and *Pictograph,* as well as *Earth Recitals: Essays on Image and Vision.* She also co-edited *I Go to the Ruined Place: Contemporary Poetry in Defense of Global Human Rights.* She has counted herself among the feminist-lesbian resistance since she was ten years old.

Peggy Landsman is the author of the poetry chapbook *To-wit To-woo* (Foothills Publishing). Her work has been published in literary journals and anthologies, including *The Muse Strikes Back, Bridges,* and *Breathe: 100 Contemporary Odes.* She is always happy to add her voice to the nasty woman chorus.

Elizabeth Lara's poems have appeared in numerous online and print journals. She was a member of the Hot Poets Collective (New York) and co-edited *The Delight Tree—An anthology of Contemporary International Poetry* (United Nations SRC Society of Writers, 2015 & 2017)

Lucinda Lawson has an MFA from Murray State University and teaches in the rural Missouri Ozarks. Her students call her "The Lawsonator" and her children call her "Queen Mama Dragon." Her husband boasts that he calls her *Woman . . .* and then runs.

Jenna Le, the daughter of Vietnamese refugees, lives and works as a physician and educator in New Hampshire. She is the author of two poetry collections, *Six Rivers* (NYQ Books, 2011) and *A History of the Cetacean American Diaspora* (Anchor & Plume, 2016).

Courtney LeBlanc is the author of the chapbook *All in the Family* (Bottlecap Press) and is an MFA candidate at Queens University of Charlotte. She loves nail polish, wine, and tattoos.

Jessica Lee is an assistant editor at *Narrative Magazine*. Her work has appeared or is forthcoming in *American Literary Review, BOAAT, DIAGRAM, Cream City Review, Phoebe, So To Speak,* and elsewhere. She lives, collages, and subverts the patriarchy in the Pacific Northwest.

Amy Lemmon is the author of *Fine Motor* and *Saint Nobody*, and co-author, with Denise Duhamel, of *ABBA: The Poems* and *Enjoy Hot or Iced.* Her work has appeared in *The Best American Poetry, Rolling Stone, New Letters, Verse, The Journal,* and elsewhere. She writes, teaches, and ferociously parents two teens in New York City.

Harriet Levin is the author of three books of poetry and a novel, *How Fast Can You Run* (Harvard Square Editions, 2016). She holds an MFA from the University of Iowa, and has won awards from Barnard New Women Poets, The Poetry Society of America, and the PEW Fellowship in the Arts.

Lynn Levin's most recent collection of poems is *Miss Plastique* (Ragged Sky Press, 2013), a Next Generation Indie Book Awards Finalist in Poetry. She teaches Creative Writing at the University of Pennsylvania and Drexel University. She is proud to be a nasty woman.

Shirley Geok-lin Lim received the Commonwealth Poetry Prize, the first for a woman and an Asian. Her poems are widely anthologized, and she's published ten poetry collections, three short story collections, three novels, and *The Shirley Lim Collection.* Her memoir, *Among the White Moon Faces,* received the American Book Award.

Ellaraine Lockie is a widely published and awarded poet, essayist, and nonfiction book author. She has authored thirteen chapbooks, several of which have won or received finalist status in contests. Ellaraine teaches poetry workshops, serves often as a contest judge, and is Poetry Editor for the lifestyles magazine *Lilpoh.*

Laura Ruth Loomis is, inexplicably, a social worker. Her fiction chapbook, *Lost in Translation,* was published by Wordrunner Press in 2016. Her poetry has appeared in *Raising Lilly Ledbetter: Women Poets Occupy the Workspace* and *Hot Summer Nights.*

Kim Lozano teaches Creative Writing for the St. Louis Writers Workshop and St. Louis Oasis, a lifelong learning organization for people over 50. Her work has been published in *Poetry Daily, The Iowa Review, Alaska Quarterly Review, The Journal, Denver Quarterly, Poet Lore, New Poetry from the Midwest,* and elsewhere.

Los Angeles-based poet **Ronna Magy** grew up in Michigan, when Detroit Bandstand danced on the black and white and Sputnik roamed the skies. Her writing appears in *Persimmon Tree, In the Questions, Trivia, Musewrite, Sinister Wisdom, Up, Do: Flash Fiction by Women,* and *Lady Business: A Celebration of Lesbian Poetry.*

Jennie Malboeuf is a native of Kentucky (and a good witch). Her poems are found in the *Virginia Quarterly Review, Oxford Poetry (UK), The Hollins Critic, New American Writing, Sugar House Review, New South, Poetry Northwest,* and *The Best New Poets 2016.* She teaches writing at Guilford College in North Carolina.

Eileen Malone's poetry has been published in over five hundred literary journals and anthologies. Her *Letters with Taloned Claws* was published by Poets Corner Press and *I Should Have Given Them Water* by Ragged Sky Press. Her sudden overnight success is due to diligence and persistent attention to craft. She is now 73 years old and still reads and writes poetry every day.

Jennifer Martelli is angry. She's been angry since November 2016. Before that, her poetry collection *The Uncanny Valley* was published by Big Table Publishing Company. Since then, Grey Books Press published her chapbook *After Bird.* She co-curates the *Vox Blog Folio* for *The Mom Egg.* And she's still pretty upset.

Since the only poem she wrote in high school was red-penciled "extremely maudlin," **Carolyn Martin** is amazed she has continued to write. Her earliest goal was to rewrite the Bible from a woman's point of view. She's still working on it and is happy to share "Resolution" as an example.

Martha McFerren received an MFA from Warren Wilson and is the author of five books, most recently, *Archaeology at Midnight*. Her poems have appeared in *Shenandoah, The Georgia Review,* and other journals and anthologies. She has not been particularly nasty of late, mainly due to lack of energy (and opportunity).

Lisa Mecham writes a little bit of everything. Her work has appeared in *Catapult,* Amazon's *Day One, BOAAT,* and elsewhere. She is proud to be a woman in all her naughty, bleeding, swollen, sticky, distasteful, intense, and blazing glory.

Jessica Mehta is a Cherokee poet and novelist. She is the author of four collections of poems, including *Secret Telling Bones, Orygun, What Makes an Always,* and *The Last Erotic Petting Zoo,* as well as the novel, *The Wrong Kind of Indian.* She's been awarded numerous poet-in-residence posts around the world.

Mary Meriam founded *Lavender Review,* cofounded Headmistress Press, and contributes to *Ms. Magazine, The Critical Flame,* and *The Gay & Lesbian Review.* Her poetry collections *The Countess of Flatbroke, The Poet's Zodiac, The Lesbian, The Lillian Trilogy,* and *Lady of the Moon* honor a cosmos of strong, creative women.

Amy Miller has worked full-time since she was seventeen, mostly in magazine and book publishing. Her work has appeared in *Camas, The Poets' Market, Rattle, Willow Springs,* and *ZYZZYVA.* Her latest chapbook is *I Am on a River and Cannot Answer* (BOAAT Press). She lives in Oregon.

Tyler Mills is the author of *Tongue Lyre,* winner of the Crab Orchard Poetry Series First Book Award (SIU Press, 2013). Her poems have appeared in *The New Yorker, Poetry,* and *The Kenyon Review.* She is editor-in-chief of *The Account* and an assistant professor at New Mexico Highlands University.

Helena Minton's poetry collections include *The Canal Bed, The Gardener and the Bees,* and *The Raincoat Colors,* a chapbook published in 2017. Her work is also included in the Lost Horse Press Anthology *Raising Lilly Ledbetter: Women Poets Occupy the Workspace.* She lives near Boston.

Nicole Miyashiro is quiet, not silent, and collecting her ekphrastic audio poems online in "Words of Art." She also writes fiction, and for the Pennsylvania Center for the Book. Her work appears in *Nailed, Lumina,* and elsewhere; can be dialed from a Telepoem Booth; and is forthcoming in *Eckleburg Review.*

Mary B. Moore's full-length collection *Flicker* won Dogfish Head's 2016 award. Her chapbook *Eating the Light* won Sable Book's 2016 contest. Cleveland State published *The Book of Snow,* also full-length, in 1998. Her work appears in *Georgia Review, Poem/Memoir/Story, Cider Press Review, Coal Hill Review, Drunken Boat,* and elsewhere.

Carolina Morales is the author of four poetry chapbooks: *Attack of the Fifty Foot Woman* (2015), *Dear Monster* (2012), *In Nancy Drew's Shadow* (2010), and *Bride of Frankenstein and Other Poems* (2008). Individual poems have appeared in *Nimrod, Poet Lore, Spoon River Poetry Review,* and other journals.

Erin Murphy is the author of six books of poems, most recently, *Ancilla.* Her poems have been published in *The Georgia Review, Field, Southern Humanities Review, Women's Studies Quarterly,* and elsewhere, and featured on Garrison Keillor's *The Writer's Almanac.* She is professor of English at Penn State Altoona.

Maria Nazos doesn't like to hear the word "no" unless she is saying it. She loves to sharply twist her radio dial and pretend it's Donald Trump's nose. Her work has appeared in *The New Yorker, TriQuarterly, The North American Review,* and elsewhere. She's perpetually annoyed by small children's laughter.

Gillian Nevers' poems have appeared in several print and online journals. She won second prize in the 2008 Wisconsin Academy of Sciences, Arts and Letters statewide poetry contest and has been nominated for a Pushcart Prize. She lives in Madison, WI, with her husband, Dan.

Lesléa Newman is the author of the poetry collections *I Carry My Mother* and *October Morning: a Song for Matthew Shepard;* the story collection *A Letter to Harvey Milk;* and the ground-breaking children's books *Sparkle Boy, A Fire Engine for Ruthie, The Boy Who Cried Fabulous,* and *Heather Has Two Mommies.*

Susan Nguyen hails from Virginia but currently lives in the desert where she is at work on her MFA in Poetry at Arizona State University.

Previous work has appeared in *PANK, diode,* and elsewhere. She is the recipient of two fellowships from the Virginia G. Piper Center for Creative Writing.

Jules Nyquist is the founder of Jules' Poetry Playhouse, LLC, a woman-owned place for poetry and play in Albuquerque, NM. She holds an MFA in Writing and Literature from Bennington College, VT. An active member of her local NOW chapter, she awaits the passing of the ERA Amendment.

Biljana D. Obradović, a Serbian-American poet, translator, critic, professor, and head of the English Department at Xavier University of LA, has published four collections of poetry, most recently, *Incognito* (WordTech, 2017). She has also published many translations and co-edited the recent anthology *Cat Painter: An Anthology of Serbian Poetry* (Diálogos Press, 2016).

Nuala O'Connor (AKA Nuala Ni Chonchúir) lives in Galway, Ireland. Her fifth short story collection, *Joyride to Jupiter,* was published by New Island in 2017. Her novel *Miss Emily,* about Emily Dickinson and her Irish maid, was longlisted for the 2017 International Dublin Literary Award.

Lyndi Bell O'Laughlin, a poet from Wyoming, was a quiet, unassuming grandmother before the recent presidential election turned her nasty. Her work has appeared or is forthcoming in several anthologies and journals, including *Blood, Water, Wind and Stone: An Anthology of Wyoming Writers* (Sastrugi Press, 2016) and *Gyroscope Review.*

Dzvinia Orlowsky is a recipient of a Pushcart Prize and an NEA for translation with co-recipient Jeff Friedman. She has published six poetry collections with Carnegie Mellon, including *Except for One Obscene Brushstroke* and her newest, *Bad Harvest,* forthcoming in 2018. Rock on, legend Donna Summers, for giving bad girls a good name.

Keli Osborn lives and curses in Eugene, Oregon, where she co-coordinates a literary reading series and works with organizations for civic involvement, equity, justice, and community resilience. Her poems appear in *Timberline Review* and *Delaware Poetry Review,* and in the anthologies *All We Can Hold* and *The Absence of Something Specific.*

Alicia Suskin Ostriker is the author of sixteen poetry collections, most recently *The Old Woman, The Tulip, and The Dog* (2014) and *Waiting for the Light* (2017). She is a chancellor of the Academy of American Poets and teaches in the Drew University low-residency Poetry MFA Program.

Melinda Palacio lives in Santa Barbara and New Orleans. Her books include the novel *Ocotillo Dreams* and the poetry collections *Folsom Lockdown* and *How Fire Is a Story, Waiting*. Her work has been featured online at the Academy of American Poets. Her third poetry collection, *Bird Forgiveness*, is forthcoming from 3: A Taos Press.

Michigan poet **Lynn Pattison's** work has appeared in *The Notre Dame Review, Rhino, Atlanta Review, Harpur Palate, Smartish Pace,* and elsewhere. She is the author of the collections of poems: *tesla's daughter* (March St. Press), *Walking Back the Cat* (Bright Hill Press), and *Light That Sounds Like Breaking* (Mayapple Press). She gets a little nastier every year.

Alison Pelegrin is a potty-mouthed, weight-lifting, born-and-raised New Orleans poet. She is the author of four poetry collections, most recently *Waterlines,* from LSU Press.

Jennifer Perrine is the author of three books of poetry: *No Confession, No Mass; In the Human Zoo;* and *The Body is No Machine.* Recent awards include the 2016 Publishing Triangle Audre Lorde Award, the 2015 Bisexual Book Award for Poetry, and the 2014 *Prairie Schooner* Book Prize in Poetry.

Valentine Pierce, artist and artisan, is always carving tree branches and stones to release poetry, writing, graphic design, sewing, and crafting from their grasp. Her piece "The Fabric of our Lives" was recently published in *Mending for Memory: Sewing in Louisiana: Essays, Stories, and Poems.*

Marge Piercy has published nineteen poetry books, most recently *Made In Detroit* and *The Hunger Moon* (selected poems) from Knopf; seventeen novels; *The Cost of Lunch, Etc.* (short stories); four nonfiction books; and a memoir, *Sleeping With Cats.* She has given readings, lectures, and workshops in over 500 venues in the U.S. and abroad.

Christine de Pizan (1364 – c. 1430) was a late Medieval author of forty-one works of poetry and prose, including *The Book of the City of Ladies* and *The Treasure of the City of Ladies.*

Hilda Raz has published twelve books of poems, essays, and criticism, as well as a memoir with Aaron Raz Link. She is editor of the Mary Burritt Christiansen Poetry Series for the University of New Mexico Press, poetry editor for *Bosque,* and founding editor of the *Prairie Schooner* Book Prize.

Nancy Reddy is the author of *Double Jinx* (Milkweed Editions, 2015) and *Barataria* (forthcoming from Lawrence Press). She is the recipient of a Walter E. Dakin Fellowship from the Sewanee Writers' Conference and grants from the New Jersey State Council on the Arts and the Sustainable Arts Foundation.

Anne Delana Reeves' work has appeared in *Image, Antioch Review, Chapter 16, The Southern Poetry Anthology,* and *Che In Verse.* She is co-editor, with Diann Blakely, of *Each Fugitive Moment: Essays, Memoirs, and Elegies on Lynda Hull* (MadHat Press). She lives in Tennessee with her beagle, Tipsy.

JC Reilly wears her pussy hat full time these days, especially when she writes poems. Her work has received a Pushcart Prize and Wigleaf nominations and is published or forthcoming in *POEM, Arkansas Review, Hawai'i Pacific Review,* and *Rabbit: a Journal of Nonfiction Poetry.*

Melanie Reitzel is an RN, International Board Certified Lactation Consultant at Stanford Children's Hospital, who comes from a long line of strong, nasty women. She earned her MFA from San Francisco State University. Her work has appeared in *Popshot, ZYZZYVA, Poet Lore, Tulane Review, North American Review, Berkeley Poetry Review,* and in various anthologies.

Christine Rhein's collection *Wild Flight* was a winner of the Walt McDonald First Book Prize (Texas Tech University Press). Her poems have appeared widely in journals, including *The Gettysburg Review, Michigan Quarterly Review,* and *The Southern Review,* and have been selected for *Poetry Daily, The Writer's Almanac,* and *Best New Poets.*

Susan Rich once put a wad of chewing gum in a camper's hair and was not sorry. Since then she's written four books of poetry, including *Cloud Pharmacy, The Alchemist's Kitchen, Cures Include Travel,* and *The Cartographer's Tongue.* She is co-editor of *The Strangest of Theaters: Poets Crossing Borders.* Awards include a Fulbright and Washington State Book Award.

Monica Rico is a second-generation Mexican-American feminist who writes at www.slowdownandeat.com. Her chapbook *Twisted Mouth of the Tulip* is forthcoming from Red Paint Hill Publishing.

Cinthia Ritchie is an Alaska writer and ultra-runner who runs mountain trails with her dog named *Seriously.* Find her work in *New York Times Magazine, Evening Street Review, Forgotten Women Anthology, Clementine Unbound, Rattle, Deaf Poets' Society,* and others. Her first novel, *Dolls Behaving Badly,* was published by Hachette Press.

Kim Roberts is the author of five books of poems, most recently *The Scientific Method* (WordTech Editions, 2017). She lives in Washington, DC, and co-edits *Beltway Poetry Quarterly*.

Alida Rol traded a career in medicine for a calmer life making poems. She lives in Eugene, Oregon, where she swears frequently, though under her breath, at the prolific and unintelligent wild turkeys who remind her of the politicians in the current regime.

Susan Rothbard's poetry has appeared in *The Literary Review, Poet Lore, The Cortland Review, National Poetry Review, Naugatuck River Review,* and elsewhere, and has been featured in Ted Kooser's *American Life in Poetry* and on *Verse Daily.* She was awarded the 2011 Finch Prize for Poetry.

Lucinda Roy is a poet, novelist, and memoirist. Her latest book is *Fabric: Poems* (Aquarius Press/Willow Books). A distinguished professor at Virginia Tech, she is working on a novel series for young adults and a series of ekphrastic poems celebrating African and Caribbean art.

Helen Ruggieri thinks the statute of limitations has expired on these crimes. She lives miles away and changed her name, so good luck finding her. She has a recent book from Mayapple Press, *The Kingdom Where No One Keeps Time.* Currently, she is working on a book called *Dead Ends,* about women who have come to one.

Linda Ruhle enjoys writing about society's taboos, death, sensuality, and the politically incorrect, and has published poetry, fiction, and nonfiction. Raised amid the redwoods of California, she loves communication, nature, photography, and practicing mental self-healing. Deliriously retired, she roams from Wyoming to California and is a full-time optimist and writer.

Pat Gallagher Sassone is a poet and novelist. Her YA novel *Hanging in the Stars* has been a hit with high school students. She has spent a lifetime in the company of many astounding women whose hard work has often been underpaid and overlooked. Why would anyone be nasty?

Lynn Schmeidler's poems have appeared or are forthcoming in numerous magazines and anthologies, including *The Awl, Barrow Street, Boston Review, Transition: Poems in the Aftermath, Drawn to Marvel: Poems from the Comic Books, Mischief, Caprice & Other Poetic Strategies,* and *Bared.* You can find her chapbooks *Wrack Lines* and *Curiouser & Curiouser* at Grayson Books.

Barbara Schmitz always wondered why our choices of female role models are either pure virgins or whores. Why can't we have sexuality and goodness combined? She has work in several new anthologies: *Bared (on breasts), Nebraska Poetry: A Sesquicentennial Anthology,* and *Watching the Perseids (20ᵗʰ Anniversary Anthology,* Backwaters Press).

One nasty thing about **Maureen Seaton** was her decision long ago to be both a mother and a poet. Killjoys along the way warned her she could not "have it all," but she persisted lovingly, poetically, nastily, and now has seventeen books and two incredible daughters. Plus, she's happy. Boo, Yah.

"Get me out of this idea" is a line from **Denise Sedman's** signature poem "Untitled," from *Abandon, Automobile* (Wayne State University Press, 2001). Architecture students at the University of Detroit-Mercy built a temporary environment in Detroit for this poem. In February, *Gravel* featured her erasure poem extracted from Donald Trump's first press conference.

Andrea Selch is the author of the safer-sex poetry series "Twentieth-Century Valentines," published by *Oyster Boy Review,* and other poems in *Calyx, Equinox, The Greensboro Review, Luna, Swank, Prairie Schooner,* and others. Her Books are *Startling* and *Boy Returning Water to the Sea.* She lives in Hillsborough, North Carolina, with her wife and two children.

Writer, critic, and micro-publisher **Elaine Sexton's** third collection of poems is *Prospect/Refuge* (Sheep Meadow Press, 2015). Her poems, reviews, and visual art have appeared in: *American Poetry Review, Art in America, O! The Oprah Magazine, Poetry,* and *Raising Lilly Ledbetter: Women Poets Occupy the Workspace.*

Martha Silano's books include *Recklessly Lovely, What the Truth Tastes Like,* and, with Kelli Russell Agodon, *The Daily Poet: Day-by-Day Prompts For Your Writing Practice.* Her poems have appeared in *Paris Review, Poetry, AGNI,* and elsewhere. Martha edits the Seattle-based journal *Crab Creek Review* and teaches at Bellevue College.

Sue William Silverman's poetry collection is *Hieroglyphics in Neon.* Her prose books include *Because I Remember Terror, Father, I Remember You; Love Sick: One Woman's Journey Through Sexual Addiction;* and *The Pat Boone Fan Club: My Life as a White Anglo-Saxon Jew.* She teaches at Vermont College of the Fine Arts.

Judith Skillman's recent book is *Kafka's Shadow* (Deerbrook Editions). Her work has appeared in *Cimarron Review, Shenandoah, ZYZZYVA, Field,* and elsewhere. Awards include an Eric Mathieu King Fund grant from the Academy of American Poets. Skillman has done collaborative translations from French, Portuguese, and Macedonian.

Janice D. Soderling has poetry, fiction, and translations in hundreds of international journals, including *Dark Horse, Glimmer Train Stories,* and *Modern Poetry in Translation.* Her writing has also received numerous prizes and awards, and is included in dozens of anthologies. She was, for many years, associate fiction editor for *Able Muse.*

Judith Sornberger has aided and abetted other nasty women by creating and teaching in the Women's Studies Program at Mansfield University of Pennsylvania. She is the author of six collections of poetry, the newest of which, *Practicing the World without You,* will be published by CavanKerry Press in 2018.

Rochelle Spencer is co-editor of *All About Skin: Short Fiction by Women of Color* (University of Wisconsin Press, 2014). She is a member of the National Book Critics Circle and a former board member of the Hurston Wright Foundation.

When **Sheryl St. Germain** sent her first poetry chapbook, *The Mask of Medusa,* to a distant relative to read, the relative sent it back, saying it was a nasty book. Since then, she has continued to write nasty books—four poetry collections, two chapbooks, and two memoirs. Her next book, *The Small Door of Your Death,* is forthcoming from Autumn House Press.

A. E. Stallings is an American poet who has lived in Greece since 1999. She named her daughter after a warrior princess who was also a huntress and athlete, because that's just how she rolls.

Margo Taft Stever's second full-length collection, *Cracked Piano,* is forthcoming from CavanKerry Press in 2019. Her chapbooks include *The Lunatic Ball, The Hudson Line,* and *Reading the Night Sky. Frozen Spring* won the 2002 Mid-List Press First Series Award in Poetry. She is founding editor of Slapering Hol Press.

Christine Stewart-Nuñez is the author of *Untrussed* (University of New Mexico Press, 2016), *Bluewords Greening* (Terrapin Books, 2016), *Keeping Them Alive* (WordTech Editions, 2010), and *Postcard on Parchment* (ABZ Press, 2008). She is an associate professor in the English Department at South Dakota State University.

Alison Stone's books include *Ordinary Magic, Dangerous Enough, Borrowed Logic, From the Fool to the World,* and *They Sing at Midnight,* which won the 2003 Many Mountains Moving Award. She was also awarded *Poetry's* Frederick Bock Prize and *New York Quarterly's* Madeline Sadin Award. She is a visual artist and psychotherapist.

Lisa Gluskin Stonestreet's *The Greenhouse* was published by Bull City Press (2014). *Tulips, Water, Ash* won the 2009 Morse Poetry Prize. Her poems have appeared in *Plume, ZYZZYVA, The Collagist, Blackbird,* and *Kenyon Review Online.* She is currently working on her third manuscript, *Annihilation,* which is quite a bit less depressing than it sounds.

A native New Yorker, **Katherine Barrett Swett** enjoys going to the opera and knitting pink hats. Recent poems have appeared or are forthcoming in *Rattle, The Lyric, Mezzo Cammin, Light,* and *Measure.* Her chapbook *Twenty-One* came out in fall 2016 from Finishing Line Press.

Marilyn L. Taylor, former poet laureate of Wisconsin, is the author of eight poetry collections. Her work has appeared in many anthologies and journals, including *Poetry, Light, Mezzo Cammin, Measure,* blah blah blah—and if you don't give a rat's ass, she would not be a bit surprised.

Tara Taylor's work can be found in *Poet Lore, River Styx, Poetry Quarterly, Nimrod, The Spoon River Poetry Review,* and elsewhere. She is a graduate of Le Moyne College and of North Carolina State University. She hopes to see the U.S. Constitution provide women with the same rights as men in her lifetime.

Kim Tedrow lives and works in Lincoln, NE, where she received her M.A. in Creative Writing from the University of Nebraska in 2016. Her poems and essays have appeared in *Prairie Schooner, Gravel,* and several anthologies. She embraces middle age as an opportunity to be authentically nasty.

Lynne Thompson is the author of *Start With A Small Guitar,* and *Beg No Pardon,* winner of the Perugia Press Prize and the Great Lakes Colleges Association New Writers Award. Thompson's poems have recently appeared in *Poetry, Ecotone, African American Review,* and *Prairie Schooner,* among others.

Allison Thorpe gives voice through poetry to women who have been silenced or who never had a chance to speak. Recent work appears in *Forgotten Women Anthology* (Grayson Books), *So To Speak, Pleiades, Roanoke Review, Pembroke Magazine,* and *Hamilton Stone Review.* She is proud to be a nasty woman poet.

Alison Townsend 's new book is *The Persistence of Rivers: An Essay on Moving Water,* winner of the Jeanne Leiby Award. She has authored two award-winning books of poems, *Persephone in America* and *The Blue Dress,* plus two chapbooks. She is professor emerita of English at the University of Wisconsin-Whitewater.

Just after the mid-point in her goody-two-shoes life, **Brigit Truex** discovered poetry and the bubble began to shatter. A later bloomer/pre-Boomer, she has relished becoming the woman she is and exploring that through writing. Expressing oneself is empowering, and doing so in this anthology gave her a large measure of comfort and strength.

Pat Valdata is a kick-ass poet and fiction writer with an MFA from Goddard College. Her poetry collections include *Where No Man Can Touch* (which won the 2015 Donald Justice Prize), *Inherent Vice,* and the chapbook *Looking for Bivalve.* Her novels include *Crosswind* and *The Other Sister.*

Jane Varley lives a fairly unsubversive life as an English Department chair and professor at Muskingum University in Ohio. However, she can get nasty when she is called "Hon" by strangers, made to feel unwelcome by good ole boys on golf courses, or when she's told to "Smile—it's not that bad."

Kathrine Varnes lives in Larchmont, NY, where she writes prose and verse when not schlepping her actor son, Henry Kelemen, to auditions, sets, and stages. Nasty is the new ethical. She is working on a collection of poems about the current U.S. administration.

Susan Vespoli comes from a long line of nasty women. Her poetry and prose have been published in various journals and anthologies, including *Mom Egg Review, New Verse News, Role Reboot,* and *Write Bloody.*

Wendy Videlock lives at the foot of the Rockies in western Colorado. Her work has appeared wildly. Some of it is nasty. Her books *Nevertheless, The Dark Gnu,* and *Slingshots* are available from Able Muse Press, and her chapbook *What's That Supposed to Mean,* from EXOT Books.

Hope Wabuke is the author of the chapbooks *The Leaving* and *Movement No.1: Trains.* She is an assistant professor of English at the University of Nebraska-Lincoln and a contributing editor for *The Root.* She has received awards and fellowships from the NEA, The *New York Times* Foundation, The Barbara Deming Memorial Fund, The Awesome Foundation, and others,

Stacey Waite is an associate professor at the University of Nebraska-Lincoln and has published four collections of poems, including *Choke,*

Love Poem to Androgyny, the lake has no saints, and *Butch Geography.* Waite's poems have appeared in *Court Green, Indiana Review,* and *Black Warrior Review.* Her newest book is *Teaching Queer: Radical Possibilities for Writing and Knowing.*

Diane Wakoski, author of *Dancing on the Grave of a Son of a Bitch,* is herself a bitch, famous for vitriolically insulting poets who win awards and honors she feels they don't deserve. Shunned by the poetry world, she has been exiled to East Lansing, Michigan, for half of her seventy-nine years.

Natasha T. Wall has published work in *The Dead Mule School of Southern Literature, Wild Goose Poetry Review, The Blue Stone Review, The Nomad,* and elsewhere. Her work reflects spiritual warnings that denote the struggle and plight of women and African Americans. She despises Trumpland, but warned people back in 2010! Her warning fell on deaf ears.

Originally from Richmond, Virginia, **Janet Lee Warman** is a professor of English and Education at Elon University. Her poems have appeared in literary magazines both nationally and internationally, and her chapbook *Lake Diving* was published by Finishing Line Press. She proudly participated in the Women's March on Washington in 2017.

Sarah Brown Weitzman's work has appeared in hundreds of journals and anthologies including *Rosebud, Miramar, The North American Review, The Mid-American Review, Rattle,* and others. She received a Fellowship for Excellence in Poetry from the NEA. A departure from poetry, her fourth book is a children's novel, *Herman and the Ice Witch* (Main Street Rag, 2011).

Gail White started being nasty in high school, where she never had a date for the prom, and continued by marrying but opting for cats instead of kids. She became a nasty poet whose works include *Asperity Street* and *Catechism,* both on Amazon. She lives in Breaux Bridge, Louisiana.

Laura Madeline Wiseman is the author of twenty-six books and chapbooks and the editor of two anthologies, including *Bared.* Her recent books are *Through a Certain Forest* and *Velocipede.* She teaches writing at the University of Nebraska and 24 Pearl Street, and writes collaboratively with Andrea Blythe.

Carolyne Wright's Lost Horse Press titles include the co-edited anthology *Raising Lilly Ledbetter: Women Poets Occupy the Workspace* (2015) and *This Dream the World: New and Selected Poems* (2017). Other books are *Mania Klepto: The Book of Eulene,* and five books of poetry in translation. Eulene foments unrest nationwide.

A Shanghai native, **Jin Jin Xu** has always lived between languages and places. Her poetry and nonfiction have been published in *Cha* and *The Common Online*. A recent graduate of Amherst College, she is currently traveling the world collecting stories of dislocated mothers on a Thomas J. Watson Fellowship.

Müesser Yeniay was born in in Izmir and has won several prizes in Turkey. Her books are *Darkness Also Falls Ground* (2009), *I Founded My Home in the Mountains* (translation), *I Drew the Sky Again* (2011), *The Other Consciousness: Surrealism and The Second New* (2013), and *Before Me There Were Deserts* (2014). She is editor of the literary magazine *Siirden*.

Andy Young's poetry collection *All Night It Is Morning* was published in 2014 by Diálogos Press. She teaches at New Orleans Center for Creative Arts and is a writer for Heinemann Publishing. Her work has appeared recently in *Voluble, One,* and *storySouth*.

Susan Yount is editor of *Arsenic Lobster Poetry Journal* and founder of Misty Publications. She works full time for the Associated Press and serves on the advisory board at The Poetry Barn. She has two chapbooks, *House on Fire* and *Catastrophe Theory*.

Andrena Zawinski's latest collection is *Landings* (Kelsey Books). Previous collections are *Something About* (Blue Light Press), a PEN Oakland/Josephine Miles Award recipient; and *Traveling in Reflected Light* (Pig Iron Press), a Kenneth Patchen competition winner. She is features editor at PoetryMagazine.com and runs the San Francisco Bay Area Women's Poetry Salon.

Barbara Zimmerman's fiction, essays, and poems have been published in numerous literary journals and anthologies, including *Rockhurst Review, Earth's Daughters, Kaleidoscope, Out of Line, The Deadly Writers Patrol,* and *New Millennium Writings,* which published her first and second prizewinning flash fictions in two separate issues.

ACKNOWLEDGMENTS

Previously unpublished poems are used by permission of the authors, who retain all rights. Grateful acknowledgment for previously published work is given to the following:

Janet E. Aalfs: "Queer": *Poem of the Moment* online, *Mass Poetry* (masspoetry.org), and *VerseWrights.com*

Nordette N. Adams: "Digital Anthropologists Find Our Hashtags": *Rattle*

Kim Addonizio: "To the Woman Crying Uncontrollably in the Next Stall": *The Night Could Go in Either Direction* (Slapering Hol Press, 2016)

Kelli Russell Agodon: "Whiskey-Sour-of-the-Nipple Waltz": *Pittsburgh Poetry Review*

Kathleen Aguero: "City Woman": *Thirsty Day* (Alice James Books, 1977)

Ann Alexander: "Clean Break": *Nasty, British & Short* (Peterloo Poets, 2007)

Patsy Asuncion: "Math for Girls Counts": *Cut on the Bias* (Laughing Fire Press, 2016)

Anne Babson: "Geraldine Ferraro Has Blood Cancer": *Lummox Journal*

Stacey Balkun: "Looking Up": *The Feminist Wire* and *Two of Cups Press Moon Anthology*, 2016. Forthcoming in *Eppur Si Muove* (Red Paint Press, 2017)

Devon Balwit: "I want to mantle my daughters' bodies": *Nailed Magazine*

Wendy Barker: "'Elegant,' She Said": *Plume*

Carol Barrett, "Milk": *Poet Lore, UECU Network,* and *Calling the Bones* (Ashland Poetry Press, 2005)

Judith Barrington, "Cavalcade": *The Conversation* (Salmon Press, 2015)

Tina Barry, "The Altos' Garage Sale": *(OINK)*

Jan Beatty, "Shooter": *Jackknife: New and Selected Poems* (University of Pittsburgh Press, 2017)

Margo Berdeshevsky, "For Sisters Everywhere, Even on St. Valentine's Day": *Before the Drought* (Glass Lyre Press, 2017)

Diann Blakely, "History": *Lost Addresses: New & Selected Poems* (Salmon, 2017)

Carolyn Breedlove, "With You Always: Iran 2009": *Just Following the River* (Finishing Line Press, 2012)

Shirley J. Brewer, "Signature": *A Little Breast Music* (Passager Books, 2008)

Jennifer Bullis, "Diana Bristles": *Rise Up Review*

Cathleen Calbert, "Bad Girl Attitude": *Cimarron Review*

Hélène Cardona, "Requiem for a Shark": *Red Sky: Poetry on the Global Epidemic of Violence Against Women* (Sable Books)

Sarah Carson, "Self-Portrait on Pop Rocks": *DIAGRAM*

Susana H. Case, "Bleached Blonde with Spiked Dog Collar": *Pittsburgh Poetry Review* and *Drugstore Blue* (Five Oaks Press, 2017)

Kelly Cherry, "Oriental Nude": *Rising Venus* (LSU Press, 2002)

Patricia Clark, "Tomboys": *Widener Review* and *My Father on a Bicycle* (Michigan State University Press, 2005)

Cathryn Cofell, "What Happens When Dad Tells Mom to Sell Her Car": *Phoebe*

Emily Rose Cole, "Leda Leaves Manhattan": *word riot*

Maryann Corbett *(translation of Christine de Pizan)* "Ballade LXXVIII": *Able Muse*

Barbara Crooker, "Women": *Les Fauves* (C & R Press, 2017)

Heidi Czerwiec, "Self-Portrait as Bettie Page: Autobioerotic": *South Dakota Review* and *Self Portrait as Bette Page* (Barefoot Muse Press)

Angela Decker, "Hair": *Cascadia Review*

Lisa DeSiro, "A Survivor Exorcises an Evil Spirit": *Prodigal's Chair*

Emari DiGiorgio, "Little Black Dress": *Compose*

Sharon Dolin, "Unpairing: Proofreading My Marriage": *Whirlwind* (University of Pittsburgh Press, 2012)

Lisa Dordal, "Plumbing the Depths": *Commemoration* (Finishing Line Press, 2012)

Amy Dryansky, "Merit Badge": *How I Got Lost So Close to Home* (Alice James Books, 1999)

Carla Drysdale, "Lifted, Carried": *The Ekphrastic Review: Writing and Art of Art and Writing*

Julie R. Enszer, "Officiant": *Avowed* (Sibling Rivalry Press, 2016)

Anna M. Evans, "Dear Sarah Rabbit": *Angie*

Alexis Rhone Fancher, "I Prefer Pussy": *KYSO Flash Fiction Journal*

Alice Friman, "The Poet": *Grist*

Nola Garrett, "The Pastor's Wife Considers Her Chops": *Georgia Review* and *Ledge* (Mayapple Press, 2016)

Emma Goldman-Sherman, "Tools": *www.prepareinc.com*

Ona Gritz, "Route 2": *Pedestal Magazine* and *Geode* (Main Street Rag, 2014)

Andrea L. Hackbarth, "The Summer We Were Thirsty": *Gravel*

Brittany Hailer, "Oprahfication": *Fairy Tale Review: The Charcoal Issue,* ed. Kate Bernheimer, Detroit, MI (Wayne State University Press)

Marie Harris, "Game": *Weasel in the Turkey Pen* (Hanging Loose Press)

Nancy C. Harris, "Ape Woman Gets an Obscene Phone Call": *The Ape Woman Story* (Pirogue Publishing, 1989)

Ashley Mace Havird, "The Harvest": *The Garden of the Fugitives* (Texas Review Press, 2014)

Karen Head, "The Other Side of the Tracks": *Loose Muse Anthology of New Writing by Women*

Amy Lee Heinlen, "Self-Portrait as the Apostle Paul": *Pittsburgh City Papers' Chapter & Verse*

Kathleen Hellen, "Love Misdemeanors": *Tampa Review online*

Sara Henning, "Other Planets, Other Stars": *Garden Effigies* (dancing girl press, 2015)

Rage Hezekiah, "Full Belly Farm": *Plainsongs*

Michele Lent Hirsch, "But How Can You Name What You Don't Have": *Rattle*

Katherine Hoerth, "Eve's Diet Advice": *Concho River Review*

Trish Hopkinson & Tyler Mills, "Waiting Around": *Wicked Banshee Press*

Rochelle Hurt, "Poem in Which I Play the Wife": *Pittsburgh Poetry Review* and *In Which I Play the Runaway* (Barrow Street, 2016)

Karla Huston, "Theory of Lipstick": *Verse Wisconsin, Express Milwaukee* (online), *Pushcart Prize XXXVI" Best of the Small Presses 2012, Verse Virtual* online, and *A Theory of Lipstick* (Main Street Rag Publications, 2015)

Elizabeth Johnston, "Delilah Scorned": *Rose Red Review* and *Tellus*

Marilyn Kallet, "Detached": *The Love That Moves Me* (Black Widow Press, 2013)

Rosalie Morales Kearns, "The Fool": *Arcana: The Tarot Poetry Anthology* (Minor Arcana Press, 2015)

Diane Kendig, "Bicycles Propped in the Garages of My Life": *3Elements Review*

Cindy King, "Mother of Invention": *Arroyo Literary Review*

Peggy Landsman, "I Remember Norman Mailer": *Spindle* and *Contemporary Literary Horizon Magazine*

Lynn Levin, "Miss Plastique": *Knockout* and *Miss Plastique* (Ragged Sky, 2013)

Ellaraine Lockie, "In the Beginning There Was": *Eastern Iowa Review* (online), *The Switchgrass Review,* and *Lumox 5*

Laura Ruth Loomis, "Hex on My Ex": *The Plastic Tower*

Eileen Malone, "Construction Worker": *Calyx*

Jennifer Martelli, "Butoh": *Vector Press*

Carolyn Martin, "Resolution": *Drash* (Northwest Mosaic, 2011)

Martha McFerren, "A Moment of Tribute": *Women in Cars* (Helicon Nine Editions, 1992)

Mary Meriam, "Liebegott": *Ocho*

Amy Miller, "I Am Over Here Sobbing": *Rattle*

Mary B. Moore, "Amanda and the Man-Soul": *PMS-PoemMemoirStory*

Erin Murphy, "Does This Poem Make My Butt Look Big?": *Too Much of This World* (Mammoth Books, 2008)

Maria Nazos, "Rock 'n Roll Fever": *The Chiron Review* and *Gargoyle*

Gillian Nevers, "Playing for Keeps": *Wisconsin People & Ideas*

Susan Nguyen, "All the Good Women Are Gone": *diode*

Jules Nyquist, "Nasty Woman Pantoum": *Duke City Sunday Fix, Poets' Speak Hers Anthology* (Beatlick Press) and *Jules' Poetry Playhouse Publications*

Nuala O'Connor, "Oh": *Tattoo: Tatú* (Arlen House, 2007)

Dzvinia Orlowsky, "Pussy Riot/Want/Don't/Want": *Plume*

Alicia Suskin Ostriker, "The Shapes of the Goddess": *the volcano sequence* (University of Pittsburgh Press, 2002)

Lynn Pattison, "You put me in the driver's seat": *Poetry East*

Alison Pelegin, "Blue Balls": *Hurricane Party* (University of Akron Press, 2011)

Jennifer Perrine, "Letter to Half a Lifetime Ago": *No Confession, No Mass* (University of Nebraska Press, 2015)

Valentine Pierce, "Handmaiden": *Geometry of the Heart*

Nancy Reddy, "Bad Magic": *Tupelo Quarterly* and *Double Jinx* (Milkweed Editions, 2015)

Christine Rhein, "Attack of the 50 Foot Woman": *Deranged: An Anthology of Women in the Arts, Rebelliousness and Gender Nonconformity* (Picaroon Poetry, 2017)

Monica Rico, "Stolen and Unnamed": *Thank You for Swallowing* and *Poet's Basement*

Kim Roberts, "IUDs": *Animal Magnetism* (Pearl Editions, 2011)

Helen Ruggieri, "The Long War": *Glimmer Girls* (Mayapple Press, 2000)

Linda Ruhle, "Glitter": *Amy Kitchener's Angels Without Wings Foundation*

Lynn Schmeidler, "My Lust": *Wrack Lines* (Grayson Books, 2017)

Maureen Seaton, "When I Was Bi(nary)": *Pank* and *Genetics* (Jackleg Press, 2012)

Martha Silano, "Wolves Keep in Touch by Howling": *Ploughshares* and *Reckless Lovely* (Saturnalia Books, 2014)

Judith Skillman, "Gaia": *Red Town* (Silverfish Review Press, 2001)

Janice D. Soderling, "Old Lesbia Reminisces over Jealous Lovers": *The Road Not Taken*

Judith Sornberger, "At Midlife, Dorothy Talks Sense to Her Daughter": *Puerto Del Sol* and *Bifocals Barbie: A Midlife Pantheon* (Talent House, 1996)

Sheryl St. Germain, "A French Mosquito Defends Itself": *Blast Furnace*

A. E. Stallings, "For Atalanta": *Five Points*

Margo Taft Stever, "Horse Fair": *The Same* and *The Lunatic Ball* (Kattywompus Press, 2015)

Christine Stewart-Nuñez, "Bad Girl": *Unbound & Branded* (Finishing Line Press, 2006)

Alison Stone, "Twat Ghazal": *Dangerous Enough* (Persea Press, 2014)

Marilyn L. Taylor, "How Aunt Eudora Became a Postmodern Poet": *Poemeleon.*

Kim Tedrow, "Tornado Dreams": *The Flat Water Stirs: An Anthology of Emerging Nebraska Poets* (WSC Press, 2017)

Lynne Thompson, "Swing Low, Free": *Spillway*

Allison Thorpe, "Jezebel Behind the Cosmetics Counter at Macy's": *Jersey Devil*

Alison Townsend, "Gospel of Jesus's Wife Revealed to Be Probable Fake": *Circe's Lament: Anthology of Wild Women Poetry* (Accents Publishing, 2016)

Pat Valdata, "Control": *Looking for Bivalves* (Pecan Grove, 2002)

Kathrine Varnes, "The Bra Burners": *Black Warrior Review*

Susan Vespoli, "I Come from a Line of Women": *Road Trip* (dancing girl press, 2015)

Wendy Videlock, "What Humans Do": *Poetry*

Hope Wabuke, "Job (War Survivor's Guilt)": *The Leaving* (Akashic Books, 2016)

Diane Wakoski: "Dancing on the Grave of a Son of a Bitch": *Dancing on the Grave of a Son of A Bitch* (Sparrow Press, 1973)

Natasha T. Wall: "Young Black Historian (Grandfather's Garage)": *Dead Mule School of Southern Literature*

Sarah Brown Weitzman: "A Poem Should Be Like Great Sex": *Miramar*

Gail White: "Pennyroyal": *Mezzo Cammin*

Carolyne Wright: "The Confessions of Eulene": *Vallum*

Andy Young: "Woman Dancing on Her Son's Coffin": *The Southern Poetry Anthology* (Vol IV: Louisiana), (Texas Review Press, 2014), and *All Night It Is Morning* (Diálogos Press, 2014)

Susan Yount: "Boys": *13 Myna Birds*

Barbara Zimmerman: "Requiem": *Earth's Daughters*